Follow us @sacred.scribe.publishing and @evokealchemy
Tag us in your images #SacredScribePublishing
www.sacredscribepublishing.com

Shadows of Tarot, Tarot Spread Journal
Published by Sacred Scribe Publishing LLC

Edited by Leah Shoman
Designs by Emma Howard
All artwork by Emma Howard

ISBN: 979-8-9909560-3-2

Printed and bound in China.

Introduction

This Journal Belongs To

Welcome to your shadow tarot spread journal.

This is a profound journey of self-reflection into enlightenment designed especially for you.

Discover various ways to delve deeply into your soul's shadows, with both basic and advanced spreads for all levels of tarot readers.

The journal is thoughtfully arranged to help you connect with your inner depths and uncover the mysteries and treasures within.

May you find clarity and wisdom throughout these pages, as you embrace the hidden aspects of yourself.

With Love Always,
Emma

Contents

Shadow Self

Taboo Shadow

Contents

Using Your Journal

This is where you will find the description of the spread you are using.

Here will be the basic spread questions

1

2

3

Choose to do the short spread or the extended version

Here you will find the extended spread questions

4

5

6

Date: ....../....../......

An affirmation relating to the spread

i.e I choose to create a day filled with kindness

What deck called to me to be used today?

i.e The Rider Waite Tarot Deck

What is my own interpretation of each card?

An area to write your card meanings

i.e Strength - I will move forward today with conviction

Ace of wands - There is potential for great success

Below you will find prompts to follow

I know that I do not take myself as seriously as I could and I should be more assertive

How does this reading inspire me to take action?

i.e I feel supported to make decisions of my own and follow through

Most prominent shadow this reading?

i.e my insecurities, this showed up twice today.

Reflective thoughts & feelings

i.e This spread told me what I knew but was in denial of.

Elemental influence

i.e I mostly had air, meaning I could be overthinking

My Long Bag

This tarot spread is a reflective journey inspired by Robert Bly's metaphor of the 'long bag,' representing parts of ourselves we choose to ignore or reject, how we are shaped by societal norms and personal experiences. By addressing each card's question, you engage with these overlooked facets, offering a pathway to greater self-awareness.

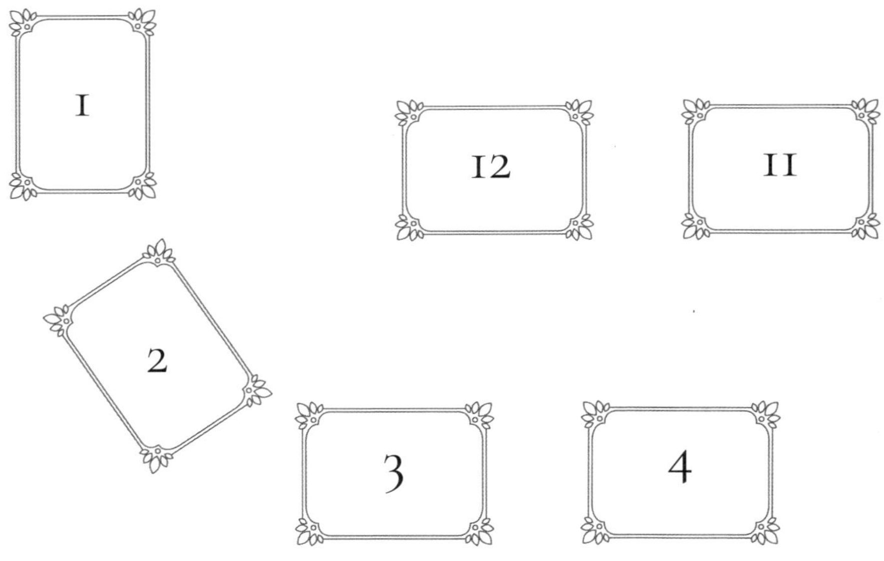

Spread questions

1 - What aspects have I unknowingly placed into my 'long bag'?
2 - Which emotions do I habitually hide in my 'bag'?
3 - What past experiences are in my 'bag' that still influence me?
4 - What hidden parts from my 'bag' manifest in my daily life?
5 - What concealed traits are packed away in my 'long bag'?
6 - What fears did I pack into my 'bag' as a child?

My Long Bag

This spread illuminates the hidden, powerful aspects of our personality that, when acknowledged, can lead to a richer, more balanced life. Through this exploration, you'll discover how these concealed traits affect your life and relationships, and how embracing them can unlock empowerment and healing.

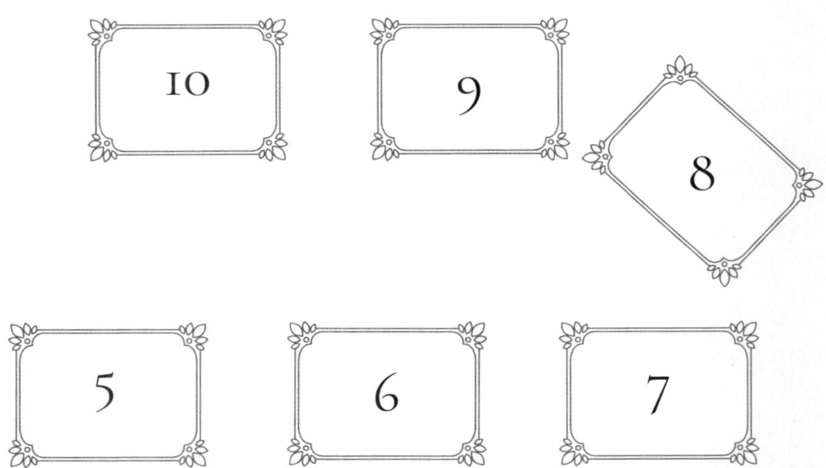

Spread questions

7 - What strengths did I hide in my 'bag' as a teen?
8 - Which aspects are ready to be seen from my 'long bag' ?
9 - What past shadows in my 'long bag' offer lessons now?
10 - How can I reveal parts of myself hidden in my 'long bag' ?
11 - What actions now will heal pieces hidden in my 'bag'?
12 - How will reclaiming myself from my 'long bag' benefit me?

Date: ....../....../......

I embrace my shadow self with love and acceptance, knowing that its presence holds valuable lessons for my evolution and advancement.

1: ....

....

2: ....

....

3: ....

....

4: ....

....

5: ....

....

6: ....

....

What currently appears to be the greatest challenge within my bag?

....

My Reflections on the treasures in my bag	What I choose to unpack
....	....
....	....
....	....
....	....
....	....
....	....
....	....
....	....
....	....
....	....

Date: ....../....../......

I welcome my shadow, acknowledging it as the keeper of treasures from my past. Each hidden part reveals lessons for my growth and empowers my journey.

7: ....

....

8: ....

....

9: ....

....

10: ....

....

11: ....

....

12: ....

....

Which repressed aspect of myself is most prominent within my long bag?

....

Echoes of introspection coming forth	Aroused responses
....	....
....	....
....	....
....	....
....	....
....	....
....	....
....	....
....	....
....	....

Shadow Self

The shadow self, refers to the unconscious aspects of our personality that are typically repressed or denied by the conscious mind.

The spreads in this quarter are designed to gently ease you into recognising the concept of having your own shadow, and what this means to you and your life.

Shadow Self Tarot Challenge

Pick one question and one card each morning for ten days.
Reflect upon the meaning and journal your thoughts in the evening.

- What part of myself do I fear the most?
- How do my shadow traits manifest in my relationships with others?
- What triggers my shadow self, and how can I manage these?
- What trauma has contributed to the formation of my shadow self?
- How does my shadow self influence my self-worth and confidence?
- In what ways does my shadow self protect me?
- What role does guilt play in the expression of my shadow self?
- How can integrating my shadow self lead to personal growth?
- What beneficial qualities can I find within my shadow?
- How can I acknowledge my shadow self with positivity?

Exploration

This spread opens the pathway to self exploration of the supressed shadow self. It is laid out in a bridge shape, symbolic of taking a path to a new destination of self.

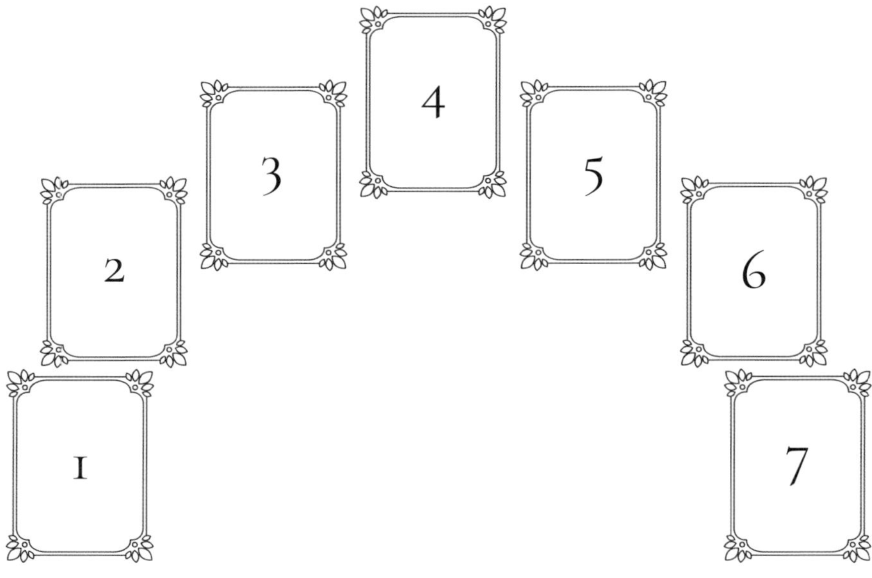

Spread questions

1 - What is the core aspect of my shadow self?

2 - What events contributed to the formation of this aspect?

3 - What subconscious influences are at play?

Extended spread questions

4 - What emotions or feelings are being suppressed?

5 - What patterns stem from this shadow aspect?

6 - What challenges will I face integrating this shadow?

7 - What steps can I take to integrate this shadow into my life?

Date: ....../....../......

I embrace and accept all parts of myself as I am without exception.

....

What deck called to me to be used today?

....

What is my own interpretation of each card?

....

....

....

....

....

....

....

....

....

....

....

....

....

How does this reading inspire me to take action?

....

....

Most prominent shadow this reading?

....

Reflective thoughts & feelings	Elemental influence
....	....
....	....
....	....
....	....
....	....

Self Healing

This spread evokes the cyclical nature of self healing and the interconnectedness of each step in the process. It emphasises wholeness, with each card representing a pivotal part of the journey towards integration and transformation.

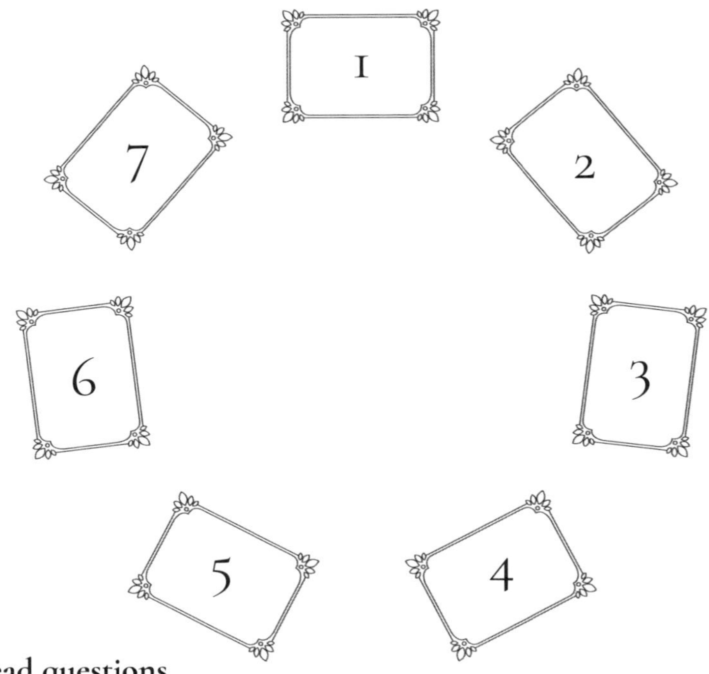

Spread questions

1 - What aspect of my shadow self requires recognition?

2 - How does this aspect see itself today?

3 - What message does this self want to share with me?

Extended spread questions

4 - What should I seek to validate about myself that I repress?

5 - Why do I avoid this healing journey?

6 - How can I begin to forgive myself?

7 - What will this healing journey help me to improve?

Date: ....../....../......

I allow my shadow self to guide my growth and healing in positive ways.

....

What deck called to me to be used today?

....

What is my own interpretation of each card?

....

....

....

....

....

....

....

....

....

....

....

....

....

How does this reading inspire me to take action?

....

....

Most prominent shadow this reading?

....

Reflective thoughts & feelings

....

....

....

....

....

Elemental influence

....

....

....

....

....

Integration

The Integration spread's downward triangle layout symbolises grounding and the flow of higher insights into daily life. The peak reveals a newly uncovered shadow aspect, while the descending cards offer steps and insights to integrate these qualities, promoting growth and balance.

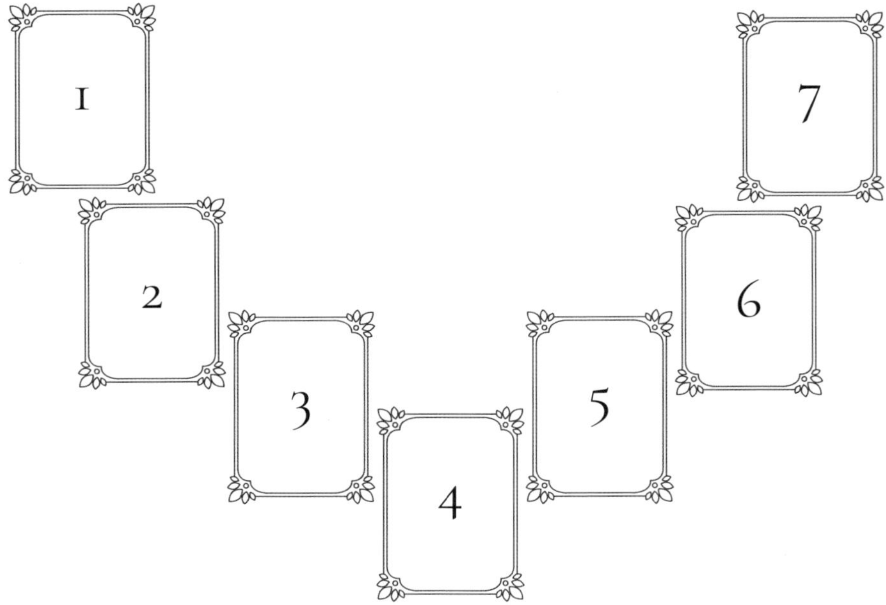

Spread questions

1 - What aspects of my shadow self have I become most aware of?

2 - How can I embrace these aspects with compassion?

3 - What steps can I take to integrate my shadow into my daily life?

4 - What lesson does my shadow self want to teach me right now?

Extended spread questions

5 - How can knowing my shadow self improve my relationships?

6 - What resources can I draw on to support this integration?

7 - How will integrating my shadow affect my well-being?

Date: ....../....../......

I lovingly integrate my shadow self, allowing its wisdom to guide my growth.

....

What deck called to me to be used today?

....

What is my own interpretation of each card?

....

....

....

....

....

....

....

....

....

....

....

....

....

How does this reading inspire me to take action?

....

....

Most prominent shadow this reading?

....

Reflective thoughts & feelings

....

....

....

....

....

Elemental influence

....

....

....

....

....

Guide Me

This spread is designed to illuminate hidden aspects of oneself. The layout's specific arrangement provides clarity and direction, harnessing a deeper self-awareness and harmonious balance between light and shadow.

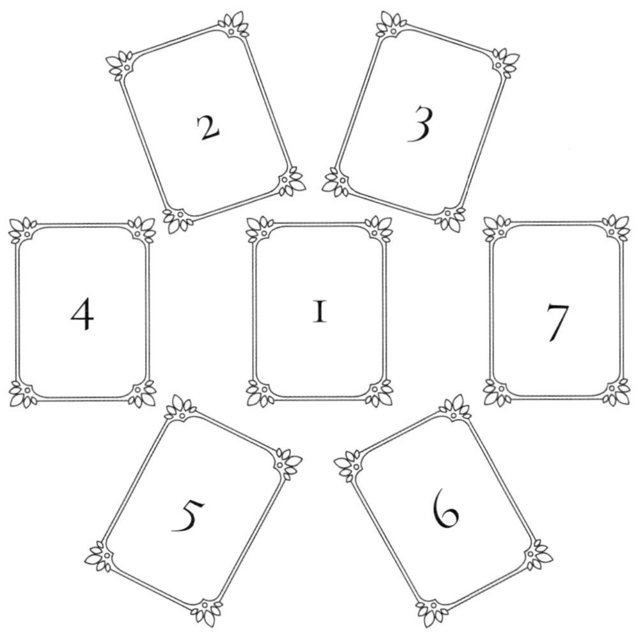

Spread questions

1 - What aspect of my shadow self am I currently denying?

2 - How does this repressed aspect impact my life?

3 - What triggers this shadow to surface?

4 - How can I begin to harmonise with this shadow positively?

Extended spread questions

5 - What emotion am I repressing?

6 - Why am I afraid of this emotion?

7 - How can I safely express this emotion?

Date: ....../....../......

I allow light to illuminate my shadow, guiding me towards wholeness and growth.

....

What deck called to me to be used today?

....

What is my own interpretation of each card?

....

....

....

....

....

....

....

....

....

....

....

....

....

How does this reading inspire me to take action?

....

....

Most prominent shadow this reading?

....

Reflective thoughts & feelings	Elemental influence
....	....
....	....
....	....
....	....
....	....
....	....

Shadowed Truths

This spread is designed to reflect both your true self and the shadow aspects of your psyche. This layout aids in unveiling hidden truths, leading to deeper self-awareness and understanding.

Spread questions

1 - What truth about myself am I hiding?

2 - Why do I feel the urge to hide it?

3 - What negative impact do I think this hidden truth has?

Extended spread

4 - How does acknowledging this truth change my perspective?

5 - How can I accept this truth?

6 - What is the outcome of accepting this hidden truth?

Date: ....../....../......

I embrace my hidden truths and reveal my authentic self with an open mind.

What deck called to me to be used today?

What is my own interpretation of each card?

How does this reading inspire me to take action?

Most prominent shadow this reading?

Reflective thoughts & feelings

Elemental influence

Hidden Depths

By exploring both your conscious and hidden traits, this spread encourages self-discovery and supports the integration of all aspects of your personality for a more holistic self-understanding. This spread has a cross layout representing the interplay between known and unknown aspects of yourself.

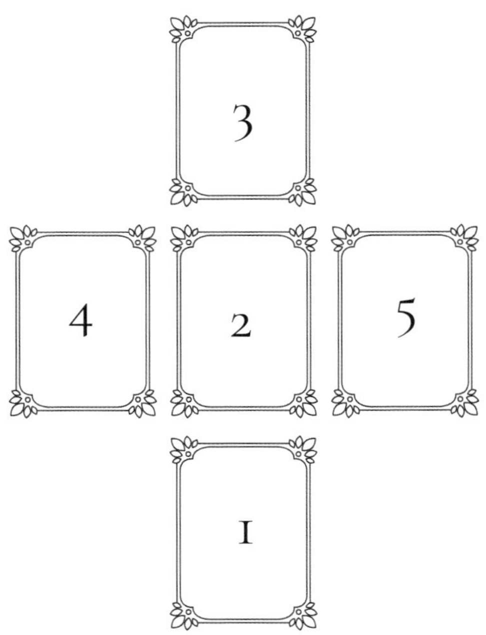

Spread questions

1 - What unknown trait lies deep within my shadow self?
2 - How does this hidden trait manifest in my daily life?
3 - What message does my shadow self have for me?
4 - How can I bring this shadow aspect to consciousness?
5 - What gift does this shadow aspect hold for me?

Date: ....../....../......

I consciously bring my hidden traits to light and embrace my complete self.

....

What deck called to me to be used today?

....

What is my own interpretation of each card?

....

....

....

....

....

....

....

....

....

....

....

....

....

How does this reading inspire me to take action?

....

....

Most prominent shadow this reading?

....

Reflective thoughts & feelings

....

....

....

....

....

Elemental influence

....

....

....

....

....

Secrets Within

This spread is designed in the shape of an arrow, symbolising the journey from darkness to light. Each card represents a step towards uncovering and understanding, ultimately guiding you towards liberation and healing.

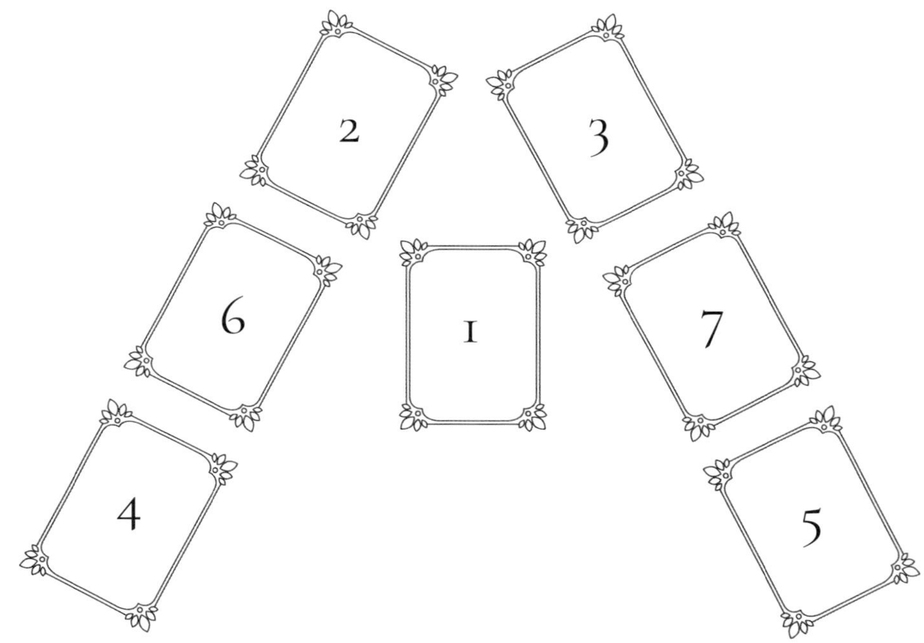

Spread questions

1 - What dark secret do I hide?

2 - Why is it important to confront this secret?

3 - How does this secret influence my behaviour?

Extended spread questions

4 - What are the fears associated with this secret?

5 - What steps can I take to reveal it?

6 - Who or what can support me in this process?

7 - What will be the benefit of confronting this secret?

Date: ....../....../......

I confront my secrets, knowing that they hold the key to my freedom and light.

....

What deck called to me to be used today?

....

What is my own interpretation of each card?

....

....

....

....

....

....

....

....

....

....

....

....

....

How does this reading inspire me to take action?

....

....

Most prominent shadow this reading?

....

Reflective thoughts & feelings	Elemental influence
....	....
....	....
....	....
....	....
....	....

My Sabotage

This staircase layout symbolises the steps to recognise and overcome self-sabotage. Each card reveals an element of your self-sabotaging behaviours, guiding you towards self-awareness and empowerment.

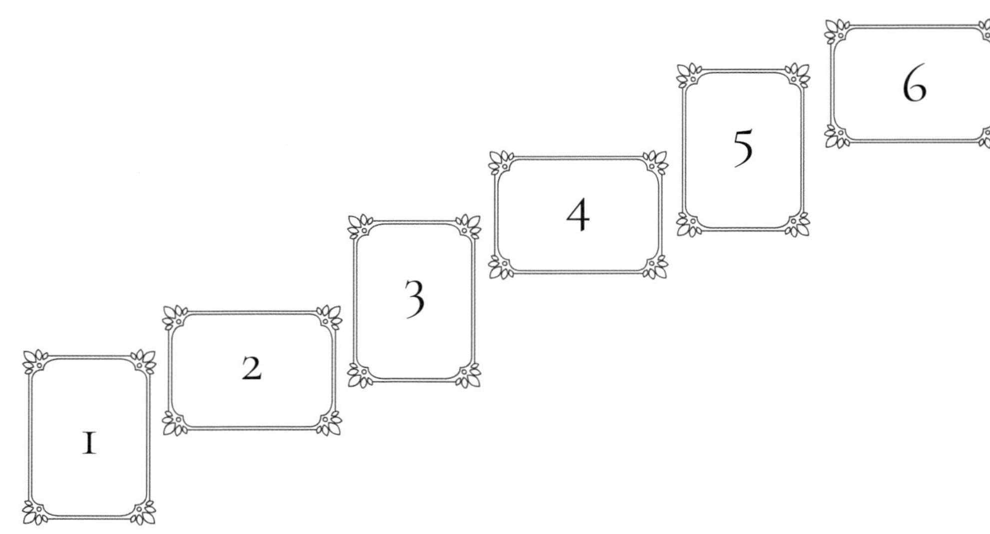

Spread questions

1 - How do I self-sabotage?

2 - What triggers this self-sabotage?

3 - How does this behaviour affect my goals?

Extended spread questions

4 - What is the hidden belief fuelling this sabotage?

5 - How can I start on the path to overcome this act of sabotage?

6 - What does my future look like if I follow my path?

Date: ....../....../......

I recognise my self-sabotage and take mindful steps towards fulfilling my life goals.

What deck called to me to be used today?

What is my own interpretation of each card?

How does this reading inspire me to take action?

Most prominent shadow this reading?

Reflective thoughts & feelings

Elemental influence

Darkest Desire

This spread delves into your hidden desires, using a flame layout to symbolise the all consuming longings into conscious realisation. Each card's position unveils layers of the self, guiding towards greater understanding.

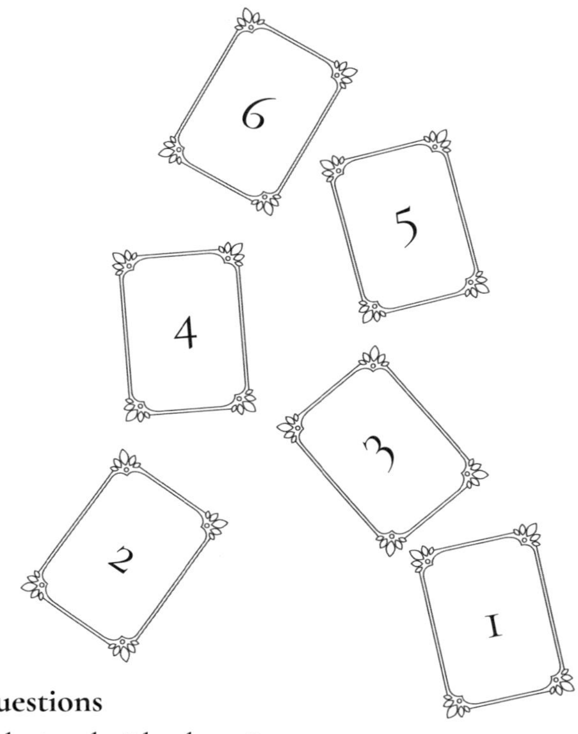

Spread questions

1 - What desire do I harbour?
2 - Why do I consider it dark?
3 - How does repressing this desire affect me?

Extended spread questions

4 - What is the true purpose of this desire?
5 - How can I channel this desire productively?
6 - What outcome can I expect from accepting this desire?

Date: ....../....../......

I ignite the flame of my desires, embracing the shadows to transform my reality.

What deck called to me to be used today?

What is my own interpretation of each card?

How does this reading inspire me to take action?

Most prominent shadow this reading?

Reflective thoughts & feelings

Elemental influence

My Imperfection

This tree-shaped spread represents the journey of self-acceptance. Beginning at the roots with your deeply held imperfections, it ascends through the trunk and branches, guiding you to a place of self-love and personal growth symbolised by the leaves.

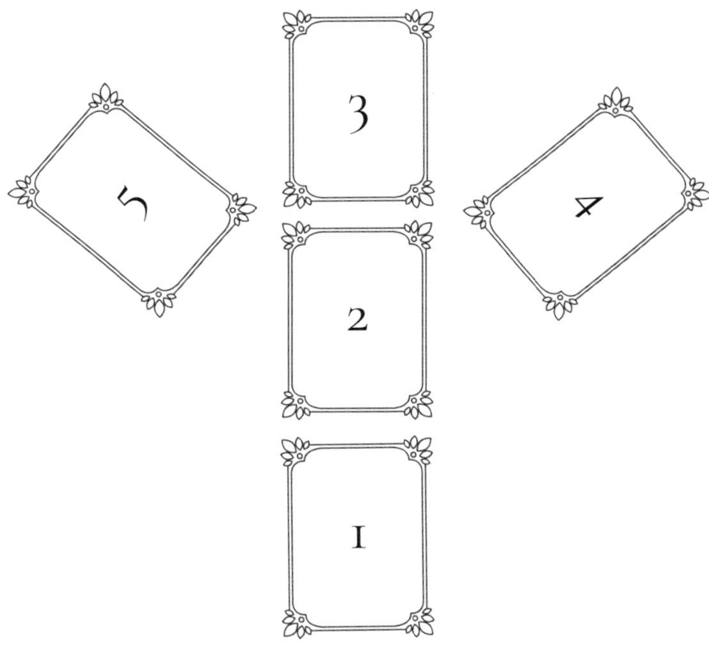

Spread questions

1 - What imperfections do I struggle to accept?
2 - How do these imperfections affect my self-esteem?
3 - Why is it important to embrace these imperfections?
4 - What can I do to accept them?
5 - How will this acceptance improve my life?

Date: ....../....../......

I am rooted in my imperfections, I grow stronger and flourish in self-acceptance.

What deck called to me to be used today?

What is my own interpretation of each card?

How does this reading inspire me to take action?

Most prominent shadow this reading?

Reflective thoughts & feelings

Elemental influence

Inner Darkness

This spread dives deep into the shadows within, guiding you through a structured exploration of fears and their transformation. The layout resembles a torch, symbolising the journey from recognising darkness to offering a clear and guided path towards integration and growth.

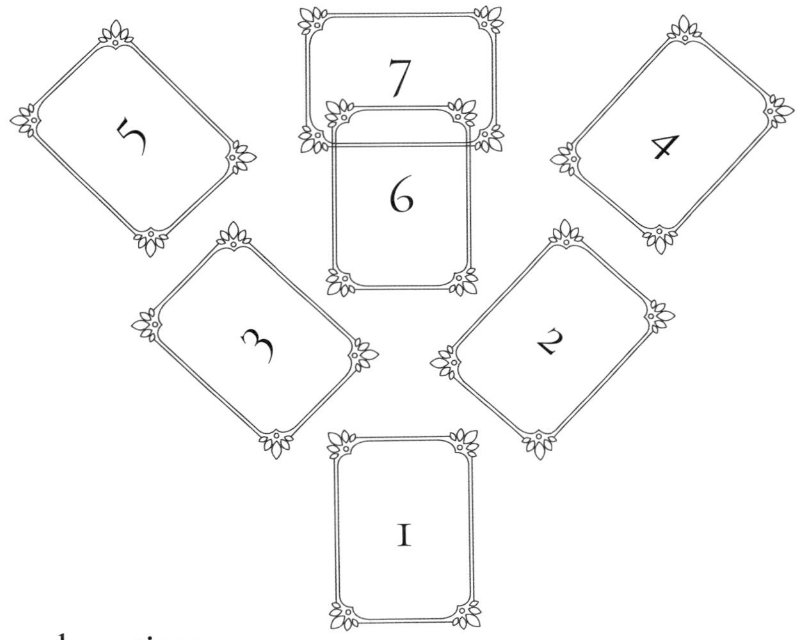

Spread questions

1 - What inner darkness do I fear?

2 - How does this darkness manifest in my life?

3 - What does this darkness teach me?

4 - How can I bring light to this darkness?

Extended spread questions

5 - What resources do I need for this journey?

6 - Who can support me in this process?

7 - What will be the result of integrating this darkness?

Date: ....../....../......

I accept my inner darkness, for it reveals the enlightened path to my true self.

....

What deck called to me to be used today?

....

What is my own interpretation of each card?

....

....

....

....

....

....

....

....

....

....

....

....

....

How does this reading inspire me to take action?

....

....

Most prominent shadow this reading?

....

Reflective thoughts & feelings

....

....

....

....

....

Elemental influence

....

....

....

....

....

The Motivation

This spread offers insight into the motivations behind your shadow actions and their impact, helping you uncover and address these influences constructively. The layout symbolises a journey from understanding the drive behind shadow actions to finding positive solutions, with the central placement of the root cause indicating its foundational role.

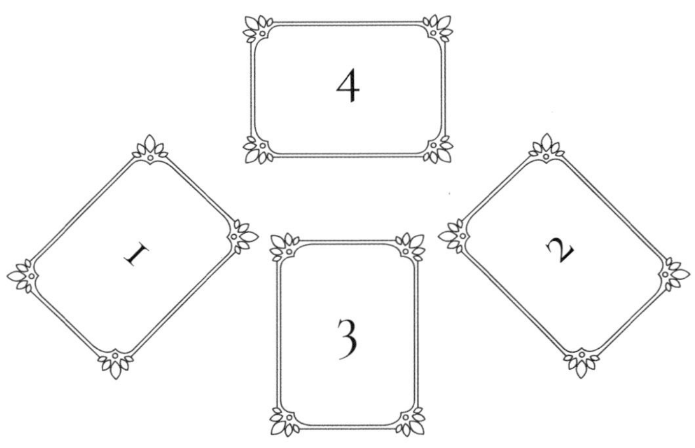

Spread questions

1 - What drives my shadow actions?

2 - How do these motivations affect my decisions?

3 - Show me the root cause of these motivations?

4 - How can I address these motivations positively?

Date: ....../....../......

I transform my shadow motivations into sources of growth and strength.

....

What deck called to me to be used today?

....

What is my own interpretation of each card?

....

....

....

....

....

....

....

....

....

....

....

....

....

How does this reading inspire me to take action?

....

....

Most prominent shadow this reading?

....

Reflective thoughts & feelings	Elemental influence
....	....
....	....
....	....
....	....
....	....

Revealing Masks

This spread helps you explore the facets of yourself that you hide behind a mask, revealing the reasons and impacts on your life. The mask-shaped layout symbolises the layered nature of your hidden self and the steps to revealing your true self.

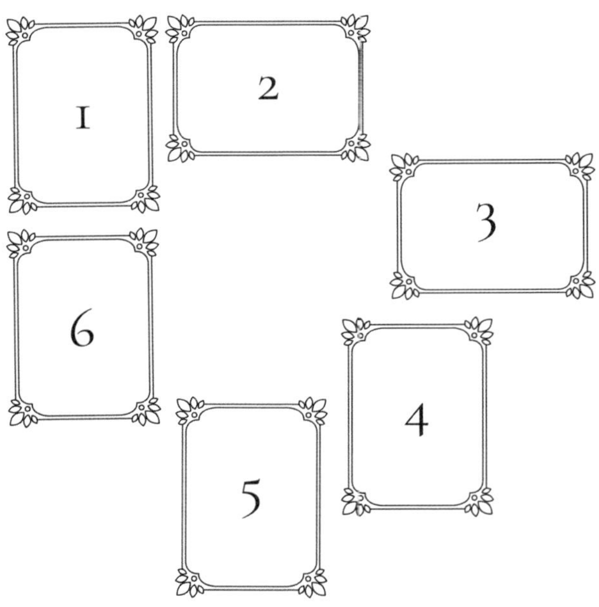

Spread questions

1 - What masks do I wear to hide my shadow?
2 - Why do I feel the need to wear these masks?
3 - How do these masks impact my current relationships?
4 - What can I do to remove these masks safely?

Extended spread questions

5 - How do I begin to reveal my true self?
6 - What changes will occur when I embrace true authenticity?

Date: ....../....../......

I am ready to remove the masks I wear and embrace my true self.

....

What deck called to me to be used today?

....

What is my own interpretation of each card?

....

....

....

....

....

....

....

....

....

....

....

....

....

How does this reading inspire me to take action?

....

....

Most prominent shadow this reading?

....

Reflective thoughts & feelings

....

....

....

....

....

Elemental influence

....

....

....

....

....

Forbidden Aspect

This spread helps you explore parts of yourself that you have deemed forbidden, providing insights into why you feel this way and how these aspects influence your daily life. The ellipse layout mirrors the process of self-acceptance, reinforcing continuity and the non-linear journey of integration.

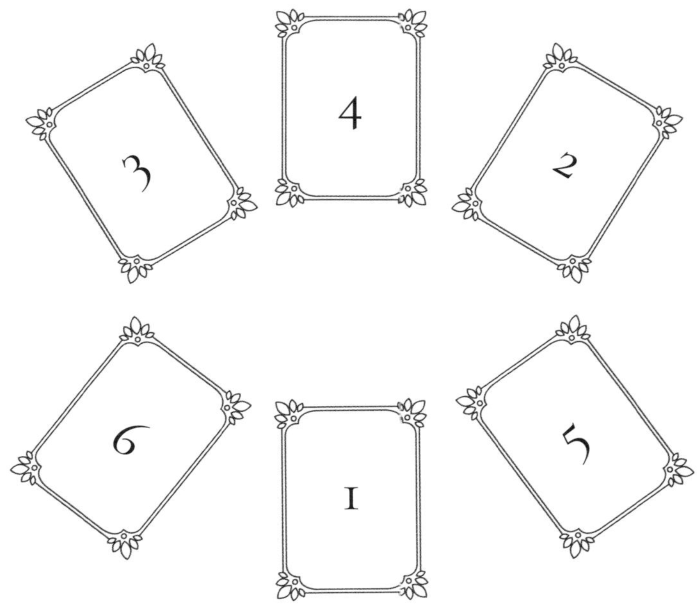

Spread questions

1 - Show me the aspects of myself I consider forbidden?

2 - Why are these aspects forbidden to me?

3 - How do these forbidden aspects affect my waking life?

4 - What would accepting these aspects look like?

Extended spread questions

5 - How can I integrate them safely and with integrity?

6 - How will life change for myself and those around me?

Date: ....../....../......

I embrace all aspects of myself, allowing each part to contribute to my wholeness.

....

What deck called to me to be used today?

....

What is my own interpretation of each card?

....

....

....

....

....

....

....

....

....

....

....

....

....

How does this reading inspire me to take action?

....

....

Most prominent shadow this reading?

....

Reflective thoughts & feelings

....

....

....

....

....

Elemental influence

....

....

....

....

....

Hidden Self

This spread guides you in uncovering hidden aspects of yourself, offering a pathway to understand why they remain concealed and how to acknowledge them. The cave-shaped layout symbolises the journey within, highlighting the process of venturing into the depths of your psyche to bring these hidden parts to light.

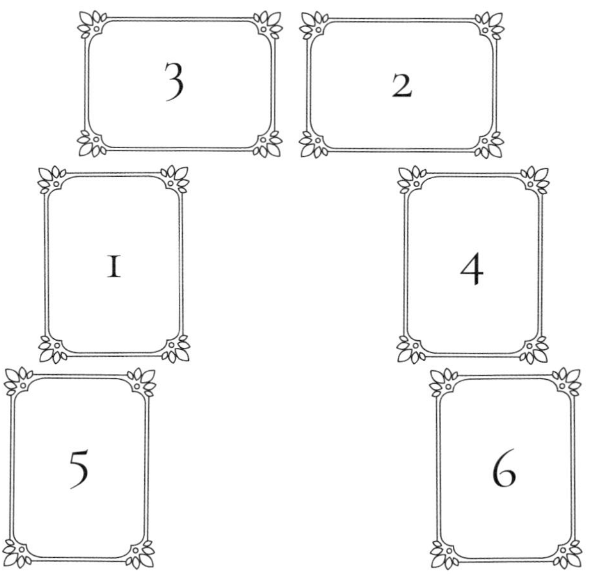

Spread questions

1 - What is concealed that I can't or won't see?
2 - Why has this part of me remained obscured?
3 - In what ways does this self seek recognition?
4 - How can I honour this part of my existence?

Extended spread questions

5 - Which fears veil my vision, preventing clarity?
6 - How can welcoming this hidden aspect enrich my existence?

Date: ....../....../......

I venture willingly into my inner depths to uncover and embrace my hidden self.

What deck called to me to be used today?

What is my own interpretation of each card?

How does this reading inspire me to take action?

Most prominent shadow this reading?

Reflective thoughts & feelings

Elemental influence

Life Narrative

This spread is laid out in a curved line resembling the horizon, symbolising the reflective journey of understanding and rewriting one's shadow self-narrative. The horizon's curve represents looking into the past as well as the dawn of new perspectives and transformative change.

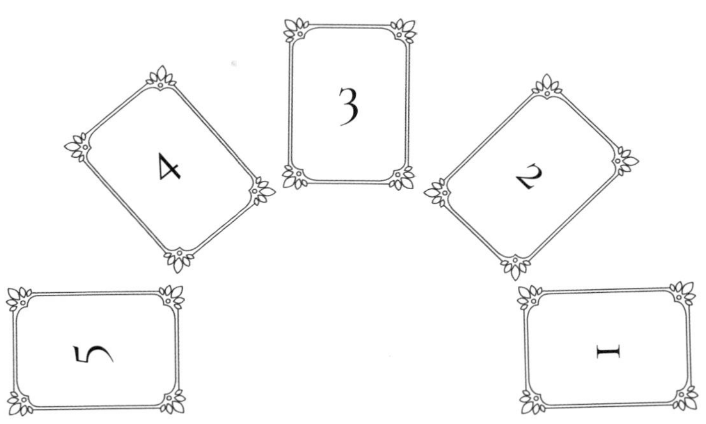

Spread questions

1 - What story do I tell about my shadow self?
2 - How does this narrative affect my life?
3 - What part of this narrative is false?
4 - How can I rewrite this story?
5 - What will change for the better when my story is rewritten?

Date: ....../....../......

I reflect on my shadows to reshape my life towards growth and enlightenment.

....

What deck called to me to be used today?

....

What is my own interpretation of each card?

....

....

....

....

....

....

....

....

....

....

....

....

....

How does this reading inspire me to take action?

....

....

Most prominent shadow this reading?

....

Reflective thoughts & feelings

....

....

....

....

....

Elemental influence

....

....

....

....

....

My Mirror

"My Mirror" invites you to creatively reflect on your shadow discoveries through drawing, mind mapping, or creative writing, capturing the insights from this section. Embrace this space to artistically express how this journey has expanded your awareness.

Date: ....../....../......

Craft a personal affirmation inspired by your reflections on the "My Mirror" page.

....

What form of creative expression did I choose today, and what drew me to it?

....

....

How do I perceive my reflection within this mirror at this moment in time?

....

....

....

....

....

In what ways has my self-perception transformed throughout this section?

....

....

....

....

....

In what ways did the revelation of my shadows defy my expectations?

....

....

....

How does this realisation of self inspire me to take action?

....

....

Shadows I recognise	Emerging insights
....	....
....	....
....	....
....	....
....	....

Taboo Shadow

The taboo shadow of the self encompasses the aspects of one's personality that are not only repressed or denied but are also deemed culturally or socially unacceptable.

The spreads in this quarter are designed to challenge your perception, recognise the value in having a moral compass and personal code of conduct and discovering how these taboo shadows came to be present in your life.

Taboo Shadow Tarot Challenge

Pick one question and one card each morning for ten days. Reflect upon the meaning and journal your thoughts in the evening.

- Which aspect of myself do I find socially or culturally unacceptable?
- Where does my taboo shadow stem from in my personal history?
- How has society influenced my perception of my shadow traits?
- In what situations do my taboo shadows reveal themselves?
- What undisclosed desires whisper to me in moments of solitude?
- What is the moral or ethical conflict related to my taboo shadow?
- How does my inner taboo shadow affect my personal conduct?
- What value can I find within my culturally repressed traits?
- How can I honour my taboo shadows while maintaining my morals?
- What steps can I take to integrate the self with compassion?

Facing Taboos

The veil layout is designed to guide you through an introspective journey from concealment to acceptance. This spread highlights the process of understanding and integrating the parts of yourself that you may regard as taboo.

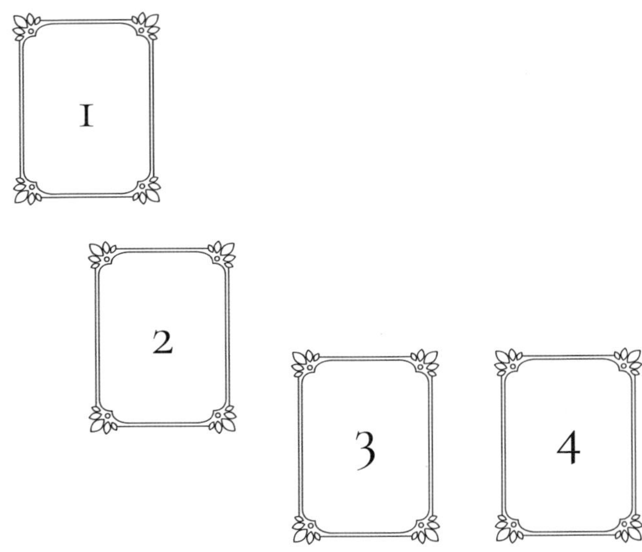

Spread questions

1 - What part of myself do I consider taboo?
2 - Why do I consciously hide this part of myself?
3 - What impact does repressing this particular taboo have on me?
4 - How can I begin to embrace and incorporate this aspect safely?

Date: ../../....

I uncover and embrace every part of myself, allowing authenticity to replace fear.

What deck called to me to be used today?

What is my own interpretation of each card?

How does this reading inspire me to take action?

Most prominent shadow this reading?

Reflective thoughts & feelings

Elemental influence

Breaking Boundaries

This spread helps you navigate societal taboos by identifying, understanding, and bridging the gap between fear and potential for personal growth. This layout resembles an arched bridge symbolising the crossing over restrictions to new freedoms.

Spread questions

1 - What societal taboo inadvertently affects me the most?
2 - How has this taboo shaped my day to day behaviour?
3 - What potential positives lie within this taboo aspect?
4 - What unexpressed fear do I need to confront about this taboo?
5 - How can I constructively express this part of myself?

Date: ....../....../......

I embrace my uniqueness and courageously cross the bridge to my true self.

What deck called to me to be used today?

What is my own interpretation of each card?

How does this reading inspire me to take action?

Most prominent shadow this reading?

Reflective thoughts & feelings

Elemental influence

Forbidden Desires

This spread invites you to gently uncover and explore your hidden desires, recognising their potential while ensuring safety and understanding throughout the journey. This layout forms the shape of a winding path, symbolising the journey through hidden aspects of desire towards newfound understanding.

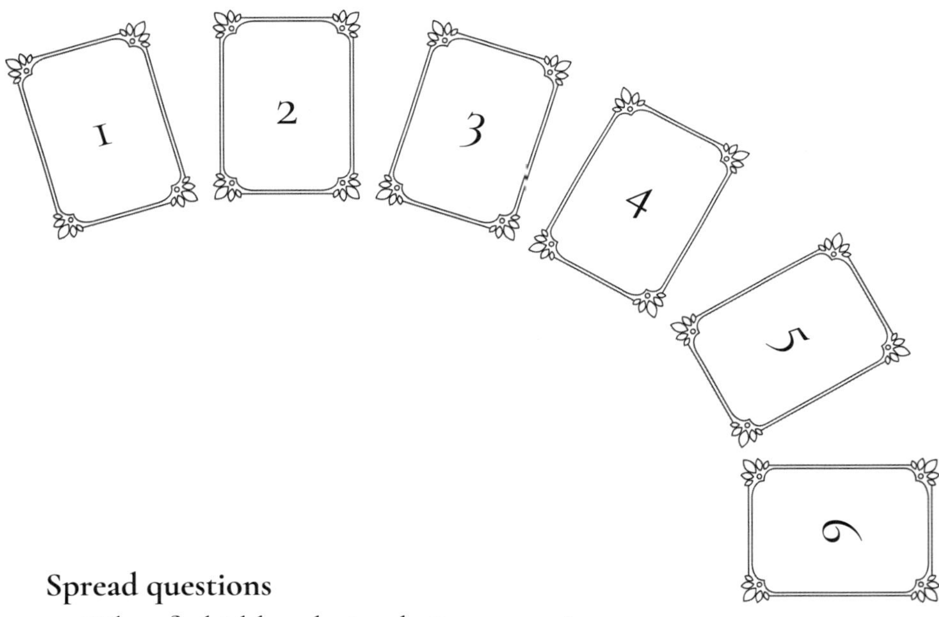

Spread questions

1 - What forbidden desire do I suppress?

2 - Why do I feel it's forbidden?

3 - What impact does suppressing this desire have?

Extended spread

4 - What potential can I unlock by acknowledging it?

5 - How can I safely explore this desire?

6 - What will be the outcome of exploring this desire?

Date: ....../....../......

I boldly walk my path, embracing hidden desires with wisdom and openness.

What deck called to me to be used today?

What is my own interpretation of each card?

How does this reading inspire me to take action?

Most prominent shadow this reading?

Reflective thoughts & feelings

Elemental influence

Breaking the Chains

This spread helps you identify and dismantle restricting beliefs, encouraging personal growth and freedom by gradually expanding your perspective. This layout spirals outward, symbolising breaking free and expanding one's horizons beyond limiting beliefs.

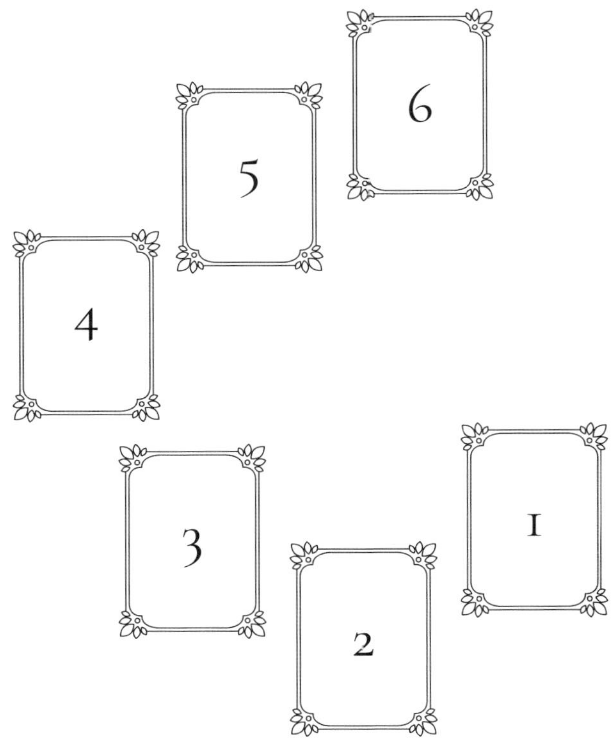

Spread questions

1 - What taboo belief holds me back from living the life I want?
2 - How does this belief affect my everyday decision making?
3 - What is the root origin of this belief?
4 - How can I begin to break free from this belief?
5 - What will change once I'm liberated?

Date: ....../....../......

I release all limiting beliefs and embrace the expansive possibilities within me.

....

What deck called to me to be used today?

....

What is my own interpretation of each card?

....

....

....

....

....

....

....

....

....

....

....

....

....

How does this reading inspire me to take action?

....

....

Most prominent shadow this reading?

....

Reflective thoughts & feelings	**Elemental influence**
....	....
....	....
....	....
....	....
....	....

Unspoken Truths

This spread encourages a gentle uncovering and release of hidden truths, helping you find peace and transparency within yourself. Laid out to symbolise the slow recognition then release of truth to the world. From unseen to seen, unconscious to conscious.

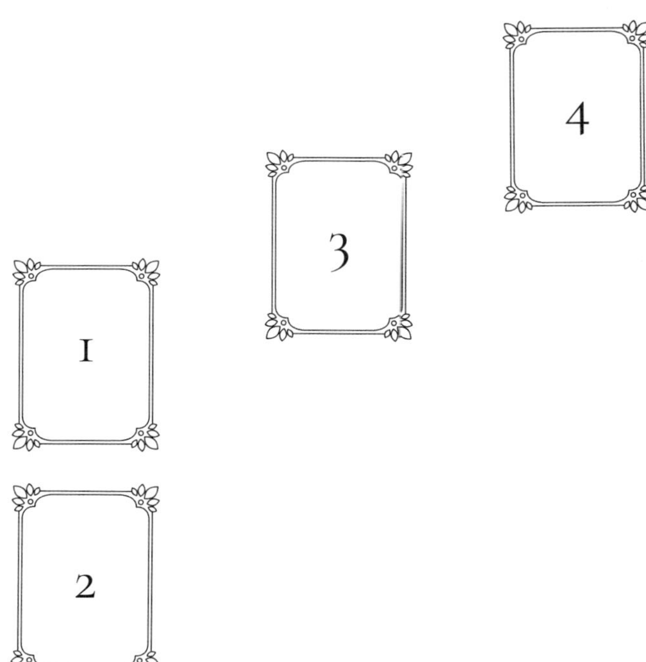

Spread questions

1 - What truth about myself do I consciously consider taboo?
2 - Why haven't I spoken this truth before?
3 - How does the secrecy I keep affect my well-being?
4 - How can I begin to speak this truth safely?

Date: ....../....../......

I embrace my truth with courage, allowing it to set me free.

What deck called to me to be used today?

What is my own interpretation of each card?

How does this reading inspire me to take action?

Most prominent shadow this reading?

Reflective thoughts & feelings

Elemental influence

Taboo Talents

This spread inspires an exploration of hidden talents, guiding you to understand their significance and the positive changes their expression could bring.

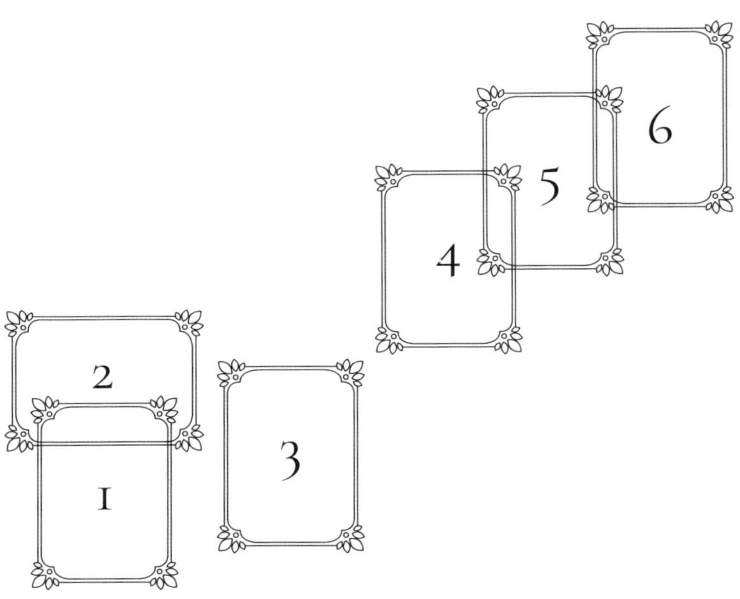

Spread questions

1 - What talent do I hide due to societal norms?

2 - Why do I consider this talent taboo?

3 - How has hiding this talent limited me in the past?

Extended spread

4 - What is the untapped potential of this talent?

5 - How can I start using this talent to its greatest benefit?

6 - What impact will showcasing this talent have?

Date: ....../....../......

My unique talents are gifts to be cherished and shared with the world.

What deck called to me to be used today?

What is my own interpretation of each card?

How does this reading inspire me to take action?

Most prominent shadow this reading?

Reflective thoughts & feelings

Elemental influence

Out of the Shadows

This four-card spread, laid in the shape of a scythe symbolising rebirth, invites you on an introspective journey from concealment to revelation. It encourages the exploration of desires and thoughts, fostering a path toward acceptance and personal growth

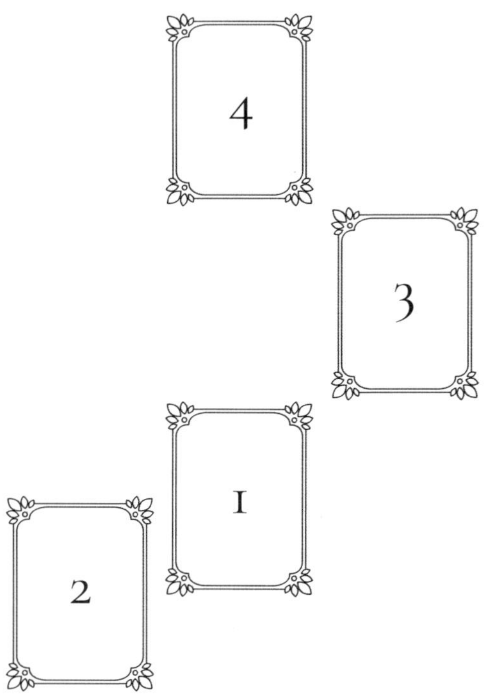

Spread questions

1 - What true aspect of myself lies dormant in the taboo shadow?
2 - How does it affect my life unconsciously from the shadows?
3 - What fear within me keeps it hidden and pushed aside?
4 - How can I bring it into the light to begin my rebirth?

Date: ....../....../......

I courageously bring my self into the light, embracing it with understanding.

....

What deck called to me to be used today?

....

What is my own interpretation of each card?

....

....

....

....

....

....

....

....

....

....

....

....

....

How does this reading inspire me to take action?

....

....

Most prominent shadow this reading?

....

Reflective thoughts & feelings

....

....

....

....

....

Elemental influence

....

....

....

....

....

Embracing Difference

This spread helps you to explore the nuances of what sets you apart, and empowers you to embrace your uniqueness, leading to personal growth and societal enrichment.

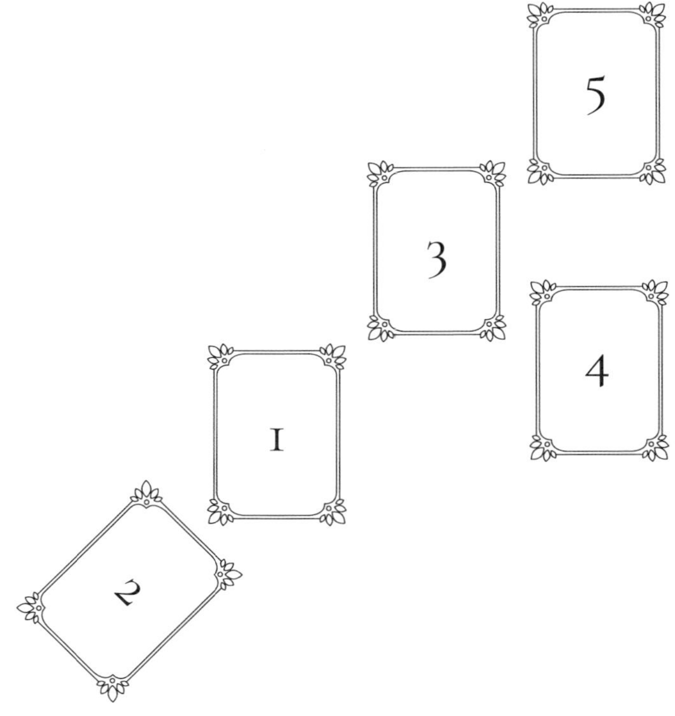

Spread questions

1 - What part of me feels different from accepted typical norms?
2 - How does this difference impact me mentally?
3 - What is valuable about this difference?

Extended spread

4 - How can I embrace this difference authentically?
5 - What will change within me when I embrace it?

Date: ....../....../......

I celebrate my differences and allow them to guide me toward fulfillment.

....

What deck called to me to be used today?

....

What is my own interpretation of each card?

....

....

....

....

....

....

....

....

....

....

....

....

....

How does this reading inspire me to take action?

....

....

Most prominent shadow this reading?

....

Reflective thoughts & feelings	Elemental influence
....	....
....	....
....	....
....	....
....	....

Defying Norms

This spread enables you to unveil the layers of restriction imposed by norms, evaluate the potential of defiance, and chart a course toward the freedom and personal satisfaction found in living authentically.

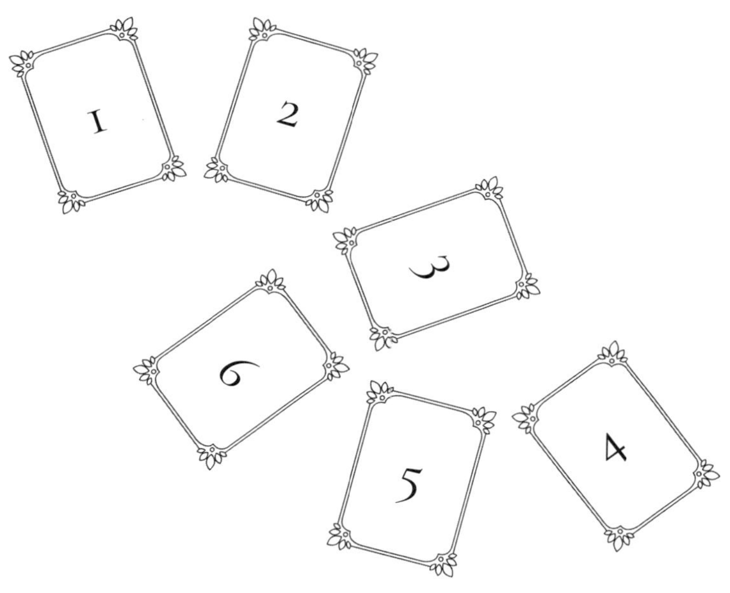

Spread questions

1 - What societal norm do I defy internally?

2 - Why do I find this norm restrictive?

3 - How does defying this norm affect me positively?

Extended spread

4 - What fear do I have about openly defying it?

5 - How can I manage the risks of defying this norm?

6 - What will be the benefit of living beyond norms?

Date: ../../....

I transcend the boundaries of societal norms to forge my own unique path.

What deck called to me to be used today?

What is my own interpretation of each card?

How does this reading inspire me to take action?

Most prominent shadow this reading?

Reflective thoughts & feelings

Elemental influence

Hidden Strengths

This spread guides you in uncovering your potent abilities shrouded by societal taboos and empowers you to integrate them openly into your life, enhancing your personal and professional world.

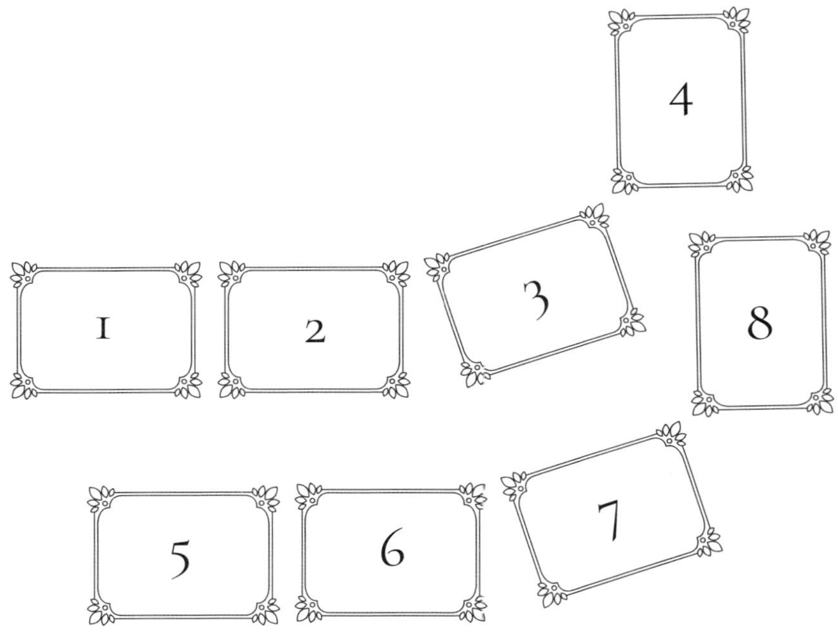

Spread questions

1 - What strength do I hide due to societal taboo?
2 - Why is this strength considered taboo?
3 - How does hiding this strength impact me?
4 - How can I reveal and use this strength?
5 - How can my hidden strengths enhance my career?
6 - How does embracing taboos spark my work innovation?
7 - What opportunities come from the unconventional me?
8 - How do my taboos shape my professional choices

Date: ....../....../......

I confidently reveal my hidden strengths, shining brightly to enrich my life.

....

What deck called to me to be used today?

....

What is my own interpretation of each card?

....

....

....

....

....

....

....

....

....

....

....

....

....

How does this reading inspire me to take action?

....

....

Most prominent shadow this reading?

....

Reflective thoughts & feelings

....

....

....

....

....

Elemental influence

....

....

....

....

....

Taboo Relationships

This spread offers insights into areas of your relationships that might be holding you back due to societal or personal taboos, fostering a journey towards greater self-acceptance and enriched connections.

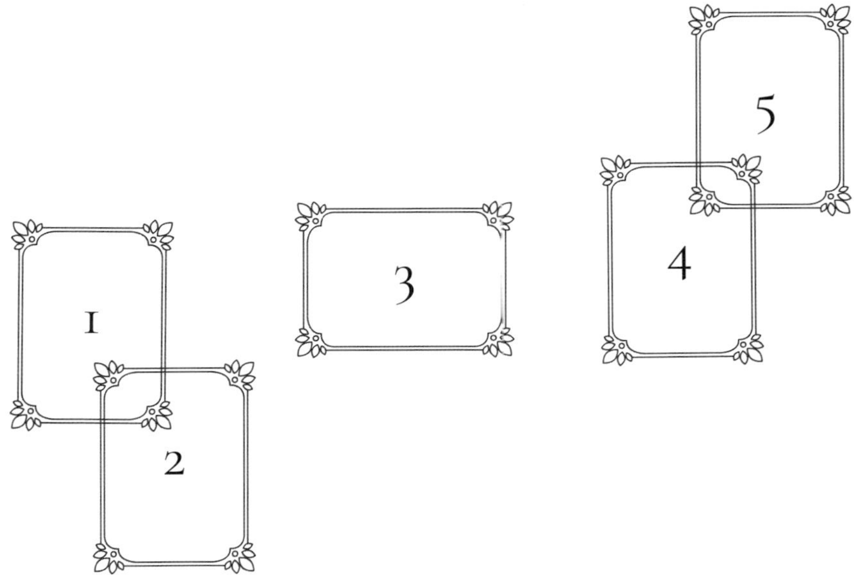

Spread questions

1 - What relationship aspect do I consider taboo?

2 - How does personal this belief affect my relationships?

3 - What would change if I accepted this aspect?

Extended spread

4 - How can I begin to accept and integrate this taboo shadow?

5 - What positive impact will acceptance have in my relationships with others?

Date: ....../....../......

I embrace the unconventional, opening my heart to life's relationships.

....

What deck called to me to be used today?

....

What is my own interpretation of each card?

....

....

....

....

....

....

....

....

....

....

....

....

....

How does this reading inspire me to take action?

....

....

Most prominent shadow this reading?

....

Reflective thoughts & feelings	Elemental influence
....	....
....	....
....	....
....	....
....	....

Forbidden Joys

This spread aids in identifying and overcoming barriers to experiencing what genuinely brings you joy, paving the way for enhanced personal well-being and authenticity.

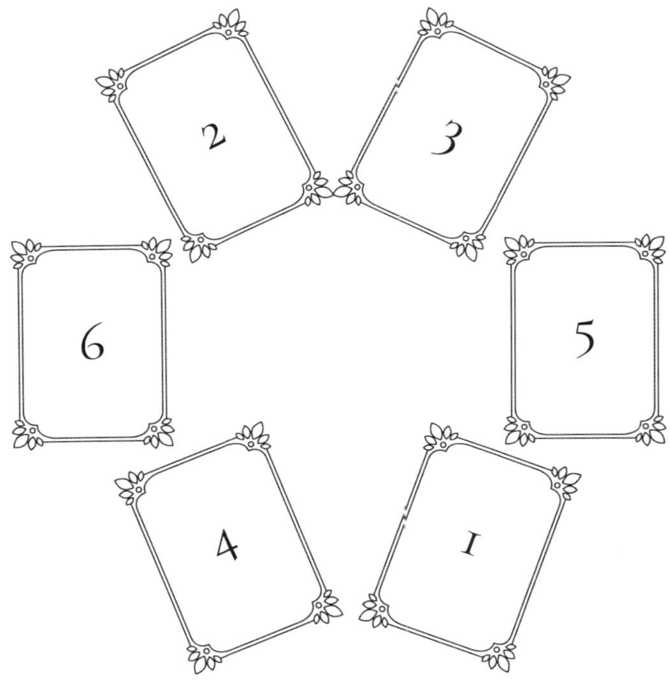

Spread questions

1 - What brings me joy that I consider taboo?
2 - Why do I suppress this joy?
3 - How does suppressing this joy affect my happiness?
4 - What fears are associated with expressing this joy?
5 - How can I safely and openly express this joy?
6 - What will change when I embrace this joy?

Date: ....../....../......

I honour my true joys, allowing them to flourish in my life and uplift my spirit.

....

What deck called to me to be used today?

....

What is my own interpretation of each card?

....

....

....

....

....

....

....

....

....

....

....

....

....

How does this reading inspire me to take action?

....

....

Most prominent shadow this reading?

....

Reflective thoughts & feelings

....

....

....

....

....

Elemental influence

....

....

....

....

....

Secrets and Lies

This spread aids in confronting how societal taboos intertwine with personal secrets and the lies we tell ourselves, guiding you toward honesty and self-acceptance.

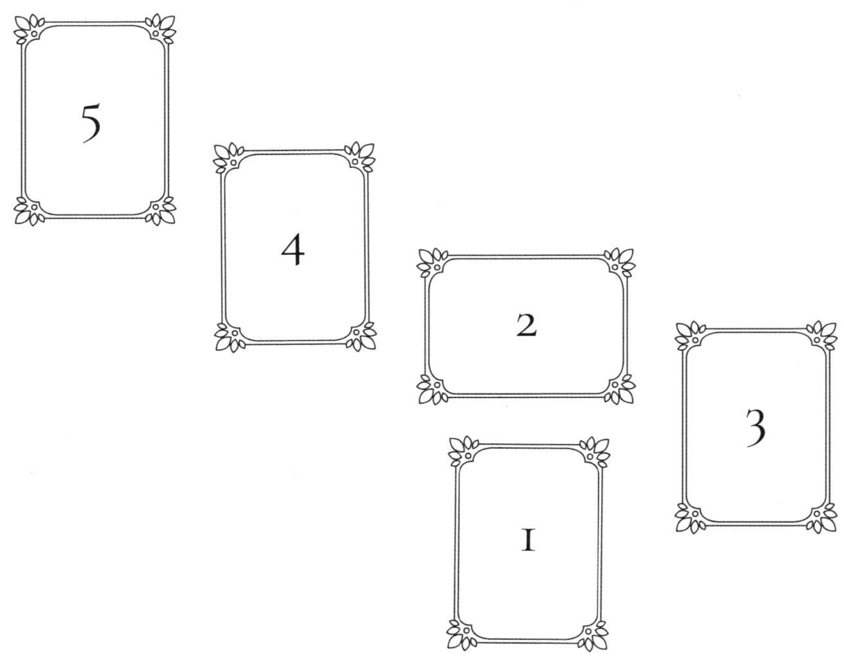

Spread questions

1 - What secret do I hold on to due to societal taboos?
2 - How does lying about this secret affect me emotionally?
3 - What is the cost to my well-being by keeping this secret?
4 - How can I start to reveal this truth?
5 - Show me a secret I am unaware of?

Date: ....../....../......

I courageously uncover my truth, embracing authenticity and freedom in my life.

....

What deck called to me to be used today?

....

What is my own interpretation of each card?

....

....

....

....

....

....

....

....

....

....

....

....

....

How does this reading inspire me to take action?

....

....

Most prominent shadow this reading?

....

Reflective thoughts & feelings	Elemental influence
....	....
....	....
....	....
....	....
....	....

Cultural Norms

This spread focuses on recognising the familial wealth and abundance shaped by cultural norms. Laid in the form of a cornucopia, it symbolises the prosperity within a family and reflects on how family expectations and the drive to uphold the family name can influence the manifestation of your own personal abundance.

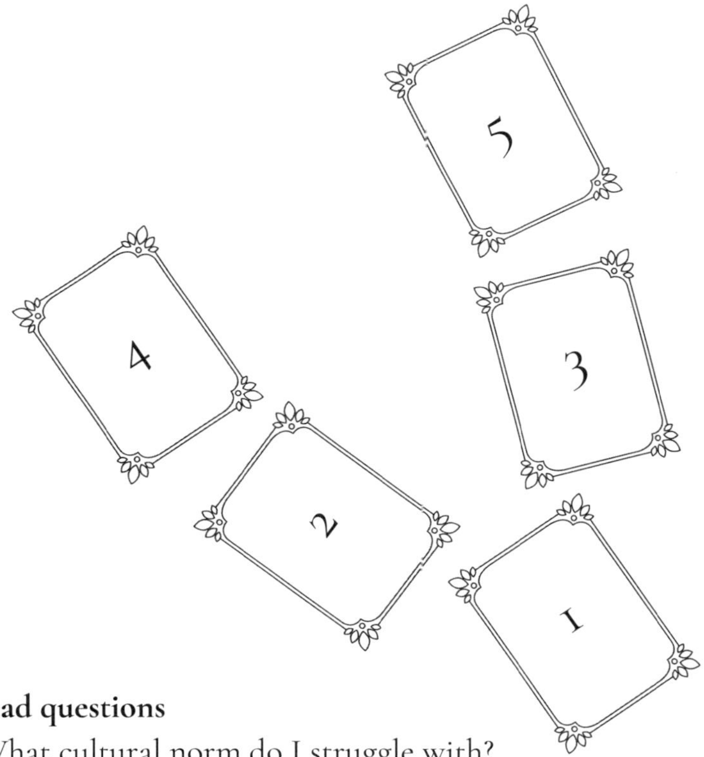

Spread questions

1 - What cultural norm do I struggle with?
2 - Why do I find this norm challenging?
3 - How does this struggle affect my outward behaviour?

Extended spread

4 - What would change if I accepted or defied this norm?
5 - How can I navigate this cultural conflict successfully in order to improve the quality of my life?

Date: ...../...../.....

I embrace the courage to understand my cultural norms with grace and integrity.

....

What deck called to me to be used today?

....

What is my own interpretation of each card?

....

....

....

....

....

....

....

....

....

....

....

....

....

How does this reading inspire me to take action?

....

....

Most prominent shadow this reading?

....

Reflective thoughts & feelings

....

....

....

....

....

Elemental influence

....

....

....

....

....

Dark Taboo

This spread empowers you to confront and understand your taboo desires, transforming them into personal strengths and enabling a more authentic expression of yourself.

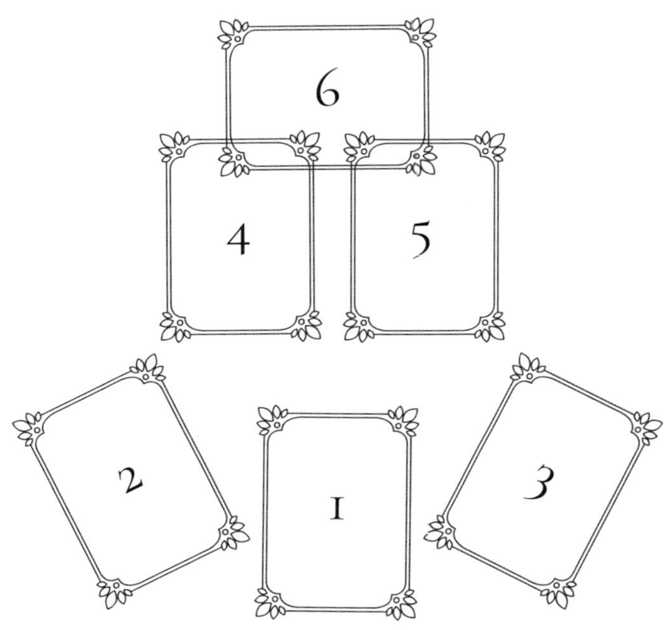

Spread questions

1 - What dark desire do I consider taboo?

2 - Why do I feel the compulsion to hide it?

3 - How does hiding this desire affect me?

Extended spread

4 - How can this desire be a source of strength to empower me?

5 - What steps can I take to safely explore this desire?

6 - What will change when this desire is acknowledged?

Date: ....../....../......

I trust in my ability to transform hidden desires into pathways of growth.

....

What deck called to me to be used today?

....

What is my own interpretation of each card?

....

....

....

....

....

....

....

....

....

....

....

....

....

How does this reading inspire me to take action?

....

....

Most prominent shadow this reading?

....

Reflective thoughts & feelings

....

....

....

....

....

Elemental influence

....

....

....

....

....

Social Masks

This spread assists you in recognising the social masks you wear, promoting self-awareness and guiding you towards a more genuine and liberated expression of your identity.

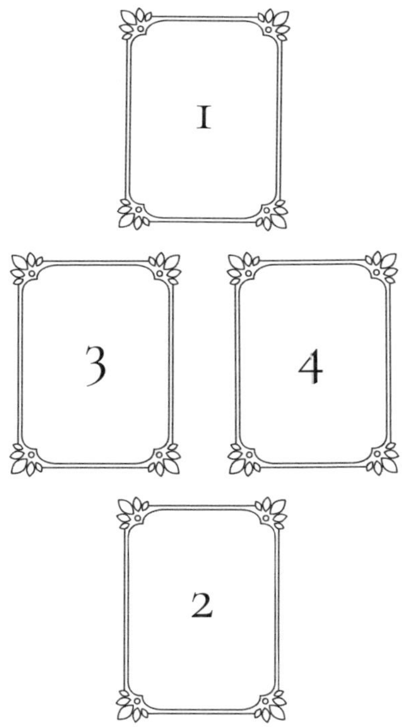

Spread Questions

1 - What social mask do I wear due to social taboos?

2 - How does this mask affect my authenticity when socialising?

3 - Why do I feel the need to wear it?

4 - How can I start to remove this mask?

Date: ....../....../......

I allow my true self to shine through, releasing the need for masks or pretenses.

....

What deck called to me to be used today?

....

What is my own interpretation of each card?

....

....

....

....

....

....

....

....

....

....

....

....

....

How does this reading inspire me to take action?

....

....

Most prominent shadow this reading?

....

Reflective thoughts & feelings

....

....

....

....

....

Elemental influence

....

....

....

....

....

My Mirror

"My Mirror" invites you to write a love letter to your taboo shadow, capturing the insights unearthed from this section. Embrace this space to express how this journey has expanded your awareness of self.

Date: ....../....../......

Craft a personal affirmation inspired by your reflections on the "My Mirror" page.

....

What taboo shadow has shown itself most prominently in this section?

....

....

....

How easily did I express my newfound awareness in my letter to my shadow?

....

....

....

....

In what ways has my self-perception transformed throughout this section?

....

....

....

....

....

In what ways did the revelation of my shadows defy my expectations?

....

....

....

How does this realisation of self inspire me to take action?

....

....

Shadows I recognise	**Emerging insights**
....	....
....	....
....	....
....	....
....	....

Mid Year Energy Check-in

This mid-year energy check-in spread examines past achievements and previews the energies of the next six months. Laid out like a person walking through an arch, it symbolises transformation and the opening of new opportunities.

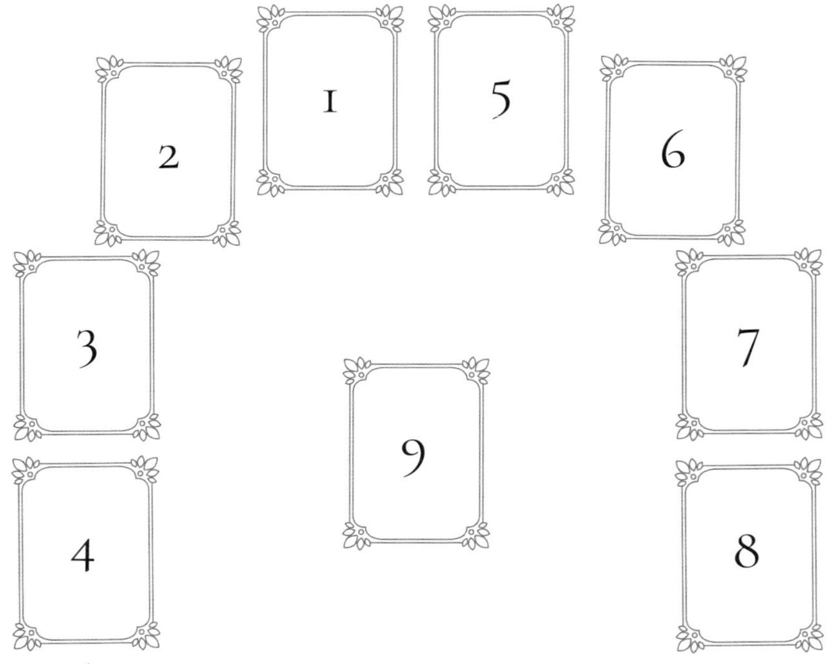

Spread questions

1 - What shadows have healed during these last six months?
2 - What action has most effectively aided this process?
3 - How has my energy become rebalanced so far this year?
4 - What will assist in grounding me during the next half-year?
5 - What should be my main goal for the upcoming six months?
6 - How can I perpetuate this success and remain positive?
7 - What shadow do I need to be most conscious of working on?
8 - What will be the most positive change coming in for me now?
9 - A message from the Universe for the next six months?

Date: ....../....../......

Each healed shadow brings me to my true self, aligned with the Universe.

....

Three emotions this spread has aroused within me?

....

What is my own interpretation of each card?

....

....

....

....

....

....

....

....

....

....

....

....

....

How does this reading inspire me to move forward?

....

....

Most prominent shadow that I have healed and nurtured so far?

....

Reflective thoughts & feelings	Elemental influence
....	....
....	....
....	....
....	....
....	....

Golden Shadow

The golden shadow of self represents the positive but unacknowledged qualities or potentials within you. These are aspects of oneself that are admired or idealised but are not fully integrated into one's conscious identity.

The spreads in this quarter are designed to celebrate you, recognise your achievements, and softly ease you into acceptance, unlocking your potential and helping you live an authentic fulfilled life.

Golden Shadow Tarot Challenge

Pick one question and one card each morning for ten days.
Reflect upon the meaning and journal your thoughts in the evening.

- What positive qualities do I admire in others but don't see in myself?
- How can I begin to acknowledge my hidden talents and strengths?
- In what ways have I underplayed my achievements?
- What traits do I possess that I need to integrate into my daily life?
- How can my golden shadow help me live more authentically?
- What steps can I take to embrace and celebrate my unique qualities?
- How have my positive traits gone unnoticed in my life?
- What benefits will I gain by unlocking my full potential?
- How can I boost my worth by acknowledging my golden shadow?
- What can help me integrate these unacknowledged shadow aspects?

Recognising Gold

This spread, arranged in the flowing path of a river, guides you through the process of uncovering and embracing overlooked personal strengths. The river's progression symbolises the journey of self-discovery, encouraging recognition, reflection, and embodiment of your golden traits.

Spread questions

1 - What positive aspect am I failing to recognise in myself?
2 - How can I start acknowledging this quality?
3 - Who mirrors this golden shadow to me?
4 - What step can I take to embody this trait more fully?

Date: ....../....../......

As I flow down the river of self-awareness, I grow and reflect.

....

What deck called to me to be used today?

....

What is my own interpretation of each card?

....

....

....

....

....

....

....

....

....

....

....

....

....

How does this reading inspire me to take action?

....

....

Most prominent shadow this reading?

....

Reflective thoughts & feelings	**Elemental influence**
....	....
....	....
....	....
....	....
....	....

Golden Potential

This spread uncovers hidden potential and guides you to embrace them for personal transformation. Laid out in the form of a rising sun, it symbolises illumination and growth.

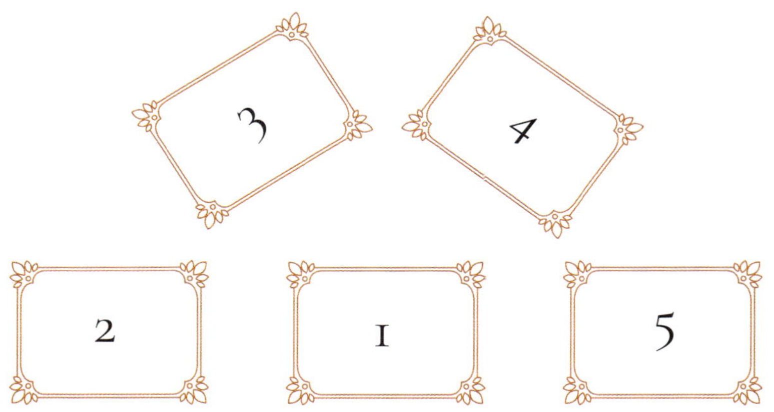

Spread questions

1 - What is my greatest hidden potential?

2 - Why do I struggle to accept this possibility?

3 - How does this strength benefit those around me?

Extended spread questions

4 - What action will help me own this gift?

5 - How will embracing this potential within transform my life?

Date: ....../....../......

I unlock the abundant potential within me, shining brightly with purpose.

....

What deck called to me to be used today?

....

What is my own interpretation of each card?

....

....

....

....

....

....

....

....

....

....

....

....

....

How does this reading inspire me to take action?

....

....

Most prominent shadow this reading?

....

Reflective thoughts & feelings

....

....

....

....

....

Elemental influence

....

....

....

....

....

My Opportunities

This spread, arranged in the form of a bridge, leads you along the path from unawareness to realisation and success. The bridge's structure symbolises the journey of recognising and seizing opportunities, supporting your transition with awareness, support, and empowered action.

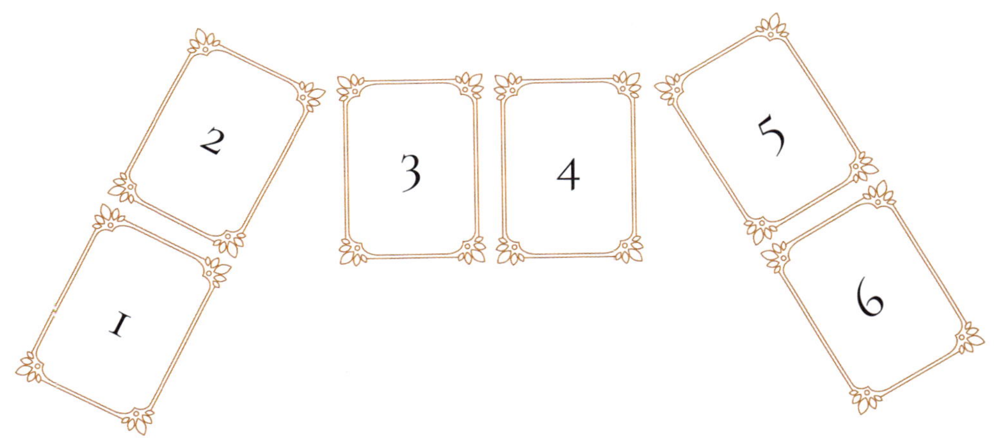

Spread questions

1 - What opportunity am I not seeing?
2 - Why do I overlook this opportunity?
3 - How can I become more aware of it?

Extended spread questions

4 - What will change when I embrace this opportunity?
5 - Who can help me seize this opportunity?
6 - What will be the outcome?

Date: ....../....../......

I am open to new opportunities and confidently step forward trusting myself.

....

What deck called to me to be used today?

....

What is my own interpretation of each card?

....

....

....

....

....

....

....

....

....

....

....

....

....

How does this reading inspire me to take action?

....

....

Most prominent shadow this reading?

....

Reflective thoughts & feelings	Elemental influence
....	....
....	....
....	....
....	....
....	....

Real Talents

This spread, arranged as a cascading flow, guides you through the gradual revelation and nurturing of your hidden talents. The cascading layout symbolises the journey towards self-awareness and empowerment, encouraging recognition, development, and expression of your innate abilities.

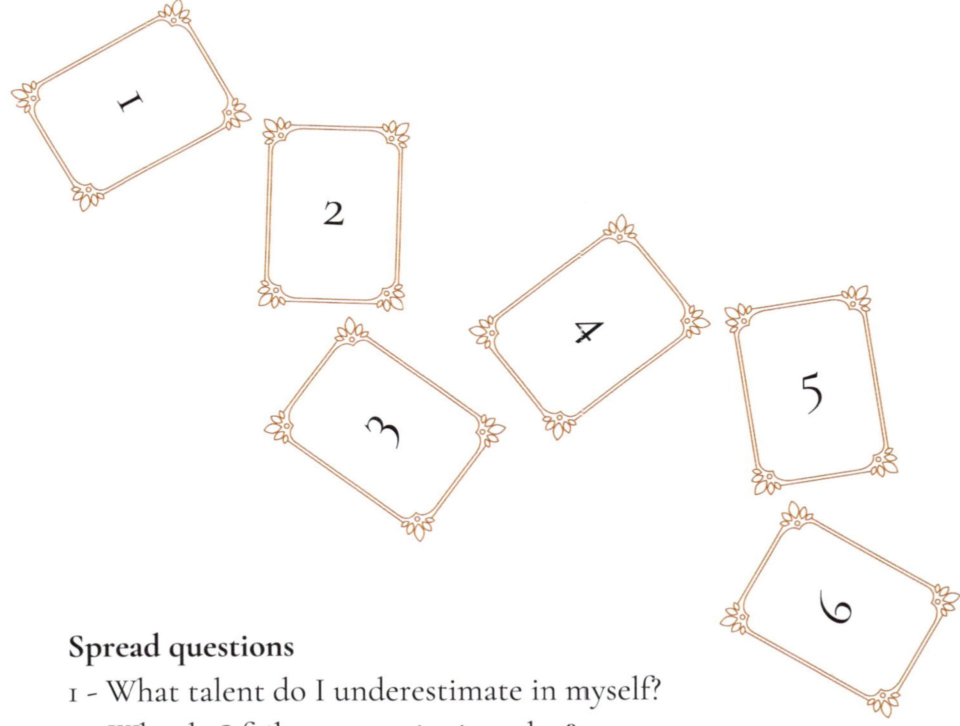

Spread questions

1 - What talent do I underestimate in myself?

2 - Why do I fail to recognise its value?

3 - How can I begin to develop this talent?

Extended spread questions

4 - What impact will expressing this talent have?

5 - What external influences have overshadowed this talent?

6 - Who can support me in fully embracing this talent?

Date: ...../...../.....

I graciously nurture my unique talents, allowing them to flow into the world.

....

What deck called to me to be used today?

....

What is my own interpretation of each card?

....

....

....

....

....

....

....

....

....

....

....

....

....

How does this reading inspire me to take action?

....

....

Most prominent shadow this reading?

....

Reflective thoughts & feelings	**Elemental influence**
....	....
....	....
....	....
....	....
....	....

Golden Gifts

This spread delves into acknowledging overlooked talents, offering insights into their subtle manifestations and future potential. Arranged in a gentle "Blooming Flower" layout, it represents the gradual unfolding of hidden capabilities for personal growth and communal benefit.

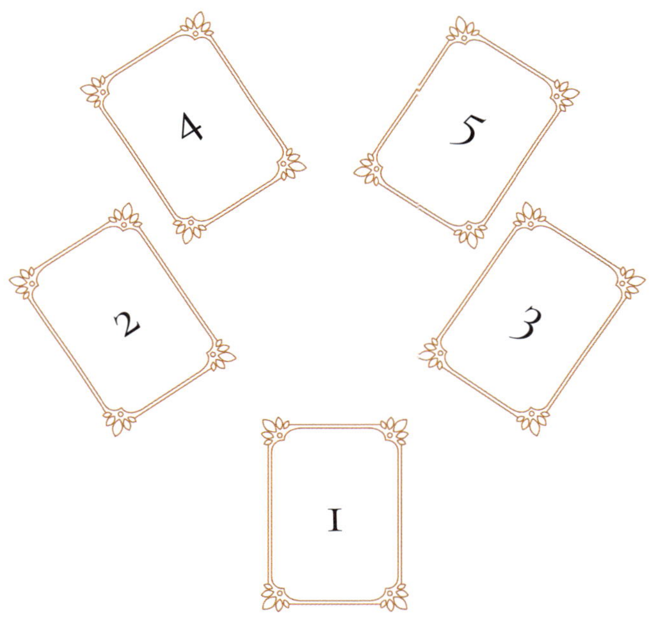

Spread questions

1 - What golden gift do I possess that I consciously ignore?

2 - How does this gift manifest in small ways?

3 - What potential does this gift hold for my future happiness?

4 - What can I do to nurture this gift in a healthy, transparent way?

5 - How will this gift benefit others when I am open to sharing it?

Date: ....../....../......

I embrace my gifts, allowing them to enrich my life and the world around me.

....

What deck called to me to be used today?

....

What is my own interpretation of each card?

....

....

....

....

....

....

....

....

....

....

....

....

....

How does this reading inspire me to take action?

....

....

Most prominent shadow this reading?

....

Reflective thoughts & feelings

....

....

....

....

....

Elemental influence

....

....

....

....

....

Positive Projections

This spread is designed to help you recognise the positive qualities you see in others that actually reflect your own potential, encouraging self-awareness and personal integration. Arranged in a "Mirror Reflection" layout, this spread symbolises the journey of internal discovery and acceptance that paves the way for embodying these traits.

Spread questions

1 - What positive trait do I unconsciously project onto others?

2 - How does this projection affect my self-perception?

3 - What does this trait in others teach me about myself?

Extended spread questions

4 - How can I reclaim this positive trait?

5 - What steps can I take to learn to embody it?

6 - What positive changes can I expect to occur when I do?

Date: ....../....../......

I embrace and reflect my innate positive qualities in everything I do.

What deck called to me to be used today?

What is my own interpretation of each card?

How does this reading inspire me to take action?

Most prominent shadow this reading?

Reflective thoughts & feelings

Elemental influence

Inner Light

This spread focuses on uncovering and acknowledging the parts of your inner self that are often overlooked, guiding you to embrace these qualities for personal empowerment. This spread is set in a radiant star, representing the illumination of your true self and the path to clarity and self-discovery.

Spread questions

1 - What inner light do I overlook?

2 - How does recognising this light begin to benefit me?

3 - What external influence blocks me from seeing it?

4 - How can I remove this block gently and with ease?

5 - How can I share my inner light gift with the world?

Date: ....../....../......

I embrace the brilliance within me, allowing my inner light to inspire my journey.

....

What deck called to me to be used today?

....

What is my own interpretation of each card?

....

....

....

....

....

....

....

....

....

....

....

....

....

How does this reading inspire me to take action?

....

....

Most prominent shadow this reading?

....

Reflective thoughts & feelings

....

....

....

....

....

Elemental influence

....

....

....

....

....

Golden Reflections

The is spread focuses on introspection and recognising past experiences that have shaped the present self. Arranged in a stepping stones layout, representing the individual steps taken through life, offering a path to deeper self-awareness and future growth.

Spread questions

1 - What do I admire in others that I possess too?

2 - Why do I struggle to see this in myself?

3 - How can I start to acknowledge this trait?

4 - What steps can I take to develop it?

Extended spread questions

5 - What significant impact will this have on my life?

6 - How can I use this trait to contribute to my community?

Date: ....../....../......

I honour my journey, acknowledging the lessons I've learned so far on the way.

What deck called to me to be used today?

What is my own interpretation of each card?

How does this reading inspire me to take action?

Most prominent shadow this reading?

Reflective thoughts & feelings

Elemental influence

Seeds Of Potential

This spread is designed to uncover dormant possibilities within you and understand how to nurture them for personal growth. Arranged in a growth path layout, it represents the journey from hidden potential to impactful change, providing clarity and direction.

Spread questions

1 - What seed of potential lies dormant within me?

2 - Why do I hesitate to cultivate it?

3 - How can I begin to nurture this seed?

4 - What support do I need for this growth?

Extended spread questions

5 - What will I gain from this growth?

6 - How will it change the behaviour of those around me?

Date: ....../....../......

I sew the seeds of my potential with intention and courage every day.

....

What deck called to me to be used today?

....

What is my own interpretation of each card?

....

....

....

....

....

....

....

....

....

....

....

....

....

How does this reading inspire me to take action?

....

....

Most prominent shadow this reading?

....

Reflective thoughts & feelings	Elemental influence
....	....
....	....
....	....
....	....
....	....

Unseen

This spread delves into hidden strengths and how to bring them to light. Arranged in a diamond layout, it symbolises the discovery and integration of unseen abilities, offering clarity and empowerment for personal growth.

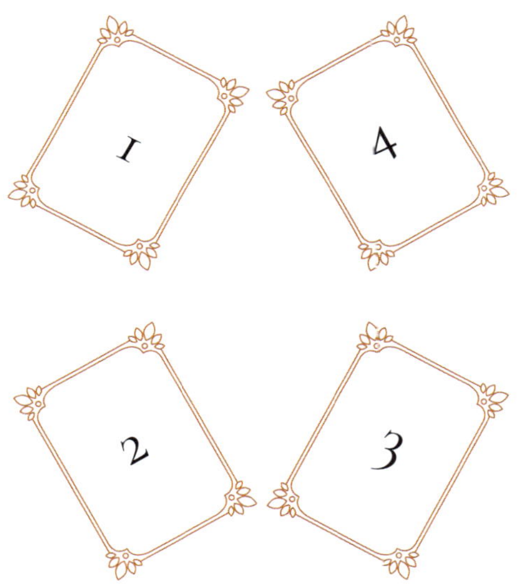

Spread questions

1 - What golden shadow do I repeatedly fail to see in myself?

2 - Why is it so hard for me to accept this particular shadow?

3 - How can I start to own and utilise this unseen treasure?

4 - What will be the impact of embracing this nugget of gold within?

Date: ....../....../......

I allow myself to embrace my hidden strengths and sparkle with clarity.

....

What deck called to me to be used today?

....

What is my own interpretation of each card?

....

....

....

....

....

....

....

....

....

....

....

....

....

How does this reading inspire me to take action?

....

....

Most prominent shadow this reading?

....

Reflective thoughts & feelings

....

....

....

....

....

Elemental influence

....

....

....

....

....

Concealed Joys

This spread delves into the hidden joys in life and offers insights on embracing them more fully. Arranged in a hidden path layout, it symbolises the journey of discovering joy that is often overlooked, bringing awareness and appreciation.

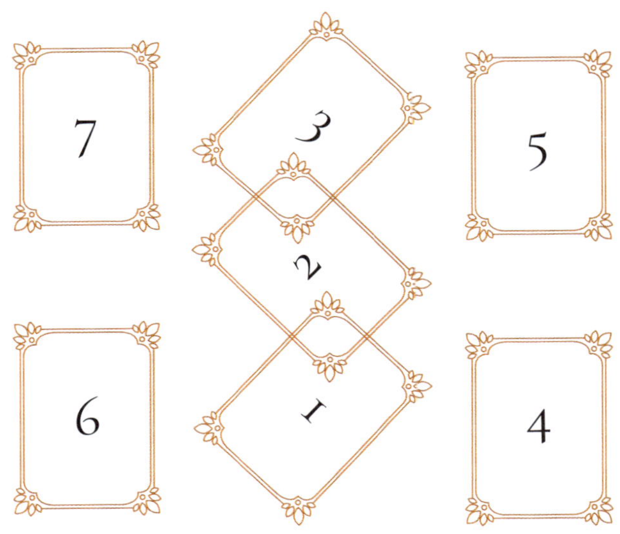

Spread questions

1 - What brings me joy that I often overlook?

2 - Why do I fail to see this joy in my waking life?

3 - How could this joy positively affect my life?

Extended spread questions

4 - How do I begin to understand it?

5 - What can I do to embrace this joy more fully?

6 - What can help me overcome this?

7 - What will change when I honour this joy?

Date: ....../....../......

I open my heart to joys flowing through me, allowing them to guide and uplift me.

....

What deck called to me to be used today?

....

What is my own interpretation of each card?

....

....

....

....

....

....

....

....

....

....

....

....

....

How does this reading inspire me to take action?

....

....

Most prominent shadow this reading?

....

Reflective thoughts & feelings	Elemental influence
....	....
....	....
....	....
....	....
....	....

Golden Relics

This spread uncovers the invaluable lessons and treasures of past experiences. Laid out in a circle, it represents the wholeness and continuity of life's journey and completion, providing insights into personal evolution and wisdom gained.

Spread questions

1 - What past achievement do I not give myself credit for?

2 - Why do I downplay this achievement?

3 - How has it shaped who I am today?

Extended spread questions

4 - What can I learn from this achievement?

5 - How can I use this lesson for my future growth?

6 - What will honouring this past achievement change?

Date: ....../....../......

I cherish the relics of my past, allowing them to illuminate my future.

....

What deck called to me to be used today?

....

What is my own interpretation of each card?

....

....

....

....

....

....

....

....

....

....

....

....

....

How does this reading inspire me to take action?

....

....

Most prominent shadow this reading?

....

Reflective thoughts & feelings

....

....

....

....

....

Elemental influence

....

....

....

....

....

Radiant Self

This spread explores the hidden aspects of your personality that shine brightly, aiming to help you acknowledge and integrate these qualities into your life. Arranged in a flame layout, it represents the heated, dynamic journey of self-discovery and empowerment.

Spread questions

1 - What part of me radiates positively that I don't recognise?

2 - Why do I overlook this radiance?

3 - How can I start to embrace this part of me?

Extended spread questions

4 - What aspect can I nurture to shine brighter in my life?

5 - How can I express my true self in my interactions?

6 - What change will this bring?

Date: ....../....../......

I embrace the hidden radiance within me, allowing my true light to shine.

....

What deck called to me to be used today?

....

What is my own interpretation of each card?

....

....

....

....

....

....

....

....

....

....

....

....

....

How does this reading inspire me to take action?

....

....

Most prominent shadow this reading?

....

Reflective thoughts & feelings	Elemental influence
....	....
....	....
....	....
....	....
....	....

Inspiring Talents

This spread reveals your inspiring talents and guides you to embrace and nurture them. Arranged in a sun burst layout, it symbolises the journey of recognising and fully embodying your talents to inspire and transform your life and others.

Spread questions

1 - What talent do I have that inspires others?

2 - Why do I overlook its true value?

3 - How does this talent of mine create positive change?

Extended spread questions

4 - What steps can I take to nurture this talent?

5 - How will fully embracing this talent transform my life?

6 - How will utilising this talent help others in the future?

Date: ....../....../......

I honour my talent's unique value, nurturing it to inspire the lives of others.

What deck called to me to be used today?

What is my own interpretation of each card?

How does this reading inspire me to take action?

Most prominent shadow this reading?

Reflective thoughts & feelings

Elemental influence

Bright Futures

This spread explores pathways to a brighter future by uncovering potential, addressing hesitations, and identifying supportive actions and allies. Arranged in a horizon layout, it symbolises the emergence of your brightest future.

Spread questions

1 - What potential future do I not allow myself to see?

2 - Why do I hesitate to envision this future?

3 - How can I begin to actively remove these barriers?

Extended spread questions

4 - What steps can I take towards this new future?

5 - Who can support and guide me on this journey?

6 - What will this future look like?

Date: ....../....../......

I embrace each step of my potential allowing it to illuminate the path ahead.

....

What deck called to me to be used today?

....

What is my own interpretation of each card?

....

....

....

....

....

....

....

....

....

....

....

....

....

How does this reading inspire me to take action?

....

....

Most prominent shadow this reading?

....

Reflective thoughts & feelings	Elemental influence
....	....
....	....
....	....
....	....
....	....

Golden Legacy

This spread illuminates the path toward leaving a meaningful and prosperous legacy.The layout resembles a golden goblet, a radiant vessel symbolising potential, success, and the vibrant life force energy that propels your legacy into being.

Spread questions

1 - What legacy am I capable of creating?

2 - Why do I doubt my ability to create this legacy?

3 - How has my journey prepared me for this legacy?

Extended spread questions

4 - What is my next step towards building this legacy?

5 - Who can help me in this process?

6 - What challenges might I face?

7 - What will be the impact of this legacy?

Date: ....../....../......

I am the architect of my destiny, reflecting the power of my journey in all I do.

....

What deck called to me to be used today?

....

What is my own interpretation of each card?

....

....

....

....

....

....

....

....

....

....

....

....

....

How does this reading inspire me to take action?

....

....

Most prominent shadow this reading?

....

Reflective thoughts & feelings

....

....

....

....

....

Elemental influence

....

....

....

....

....

My Mirror

"My Mirror" invites you to craft a collage of words and symbols that represent your golden shadows, your strengths and talents. Watch how they interweave to reveal your powerful identity.

Date: ....../....../......

Craft a personal affirmation inspired by your reflections on the "My Mirror" page.

....

What sensations arose within me as I affirmed my golden shadow in the mirror?

....

....

How do I view my reflection in the mirror right now?

....

....

....

....

....

In what ways has my self-perception transformed throughout this section?

....

....

....

....

....

In what way did the discovery of my golden shadows defy my expectations?

....

....

....

How does this realisation of self inspire me to take action?

....

....

Shadows I recognise	Emerging insights
....	....
....	....
....	....
....	....
....	....

Enlightenment

The enlightenment of self speaks to a stage of profound spiritual or personal growth characterised by heightened awareness, insight, and inner peace. Individuals often experience a deep sense of connection to the universe or a higher power, as well as a profound understanding of the interconnectedness of all things.

The spreads in this quarter are designed to bring you to a place of growth, transformation, greater self-awareness and personal fulfilment.

Enlightenment Tarot Challenge

Pick one question and one card each morning for ten days.
Reflect upon the meaning and journal your thoughts in the evening.

- What steps can I take to reach a higher state of awareness?
- How can I cultivate a deeper connection to the universe?
- In what ways can I achieve inner peace and tranquility?
- What transformations are necessary for my spiritual growth?
- How can I enhance my understanding of the interconnectedness of all things?
- What daily practices can help me maintain a state of enlightenment?
- How do I recognise moments of profound insight in my life?
- What blocks or obstacles prevent my spiritual or personal growth?
- How can I integrate greater self-awareness into my everyday actions?
- What does fulfilment look like for me and how can I achieve it?

The Path

This spread seeks to illuminate your journey towards greater self-awareness and enlightenment. Arranged in a lantern, the cards symbolise the desire for personal growth, and the energy required to follow your own path.

Spread questions

1 - What is my current level of self-awareness?
2 - What aspect of myself needs more illumination?
3 - What internal obstacle hinders my self-awareness?
4 - What can I do to enhance my path to enlightenment?
5 - What is most important to me right now?

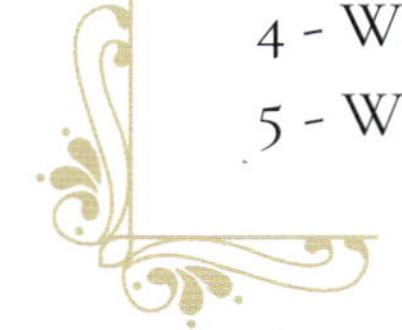

Date: ....../....../......

I shine brightly from within, lighting the path to my higher self.

....

What deck called to me to be used today?

....

What is my own interpretation of each card?

....

....

....

....

....

....

....

....

....

....

....

....

....

How does this reading inspire me to take action?

....

....

Most profound message this reading?

....

Reflective thoughts & feelings	Elemental influence
....	....
....	....
....	....
....	....
....	....

Wholeness

This spread explores the interconnected aspects of your being, helping you to embrace and integrate each part into a unified whole. Arranged in a tree of wholeness layout, it symbolises growth, balance, and unity.

Spread questions

1 - What part of myself do I need to accept?

2 - How can I better integrate my shadow aspects?

3 - What wisdom do I need to gain for enlightenment?

Extended spread

4 - What external resource can support my journey?

5 - What do I expect to achieve from this enlightened journey?

6 - What will be the outcome of achieving greater self-awareness?

Date: ....../....../......

I nurture and unite all parts of myself with love and understanding.

....

What deck called to me to be used today?

....

What is my own interpretation of each card?

....

....

....

....

....

....

....

....

....

....

....

....

....

How does this reading inspire me to take action?

....

....

Most profound message this reading?

....

Reflective thoughts & feelings	Elemental influence
....	....
....	....
....	....
....	....
....	....

I Am Light

This spread illuminates the journey to inner light and wisdom, helping you uncover the depths of your enlightenment. Arranged in a lighthouse beacon Layout, it symbolises the beacon of light guiding you through the seas of self-discovery.

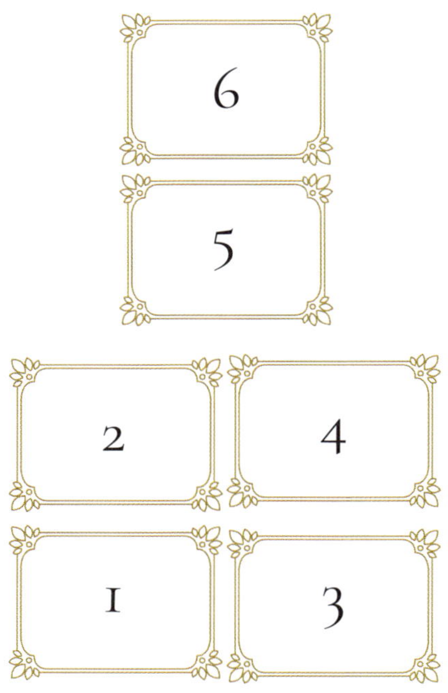

Spread questions

1 - What is blocking my path to enlightenment?

2 - What lesson do I need to learn?

3 - How can I overcome this block?

4 - What will be the benefit of learning this lesson?

Extended spread

5 - Who can I look to for support on this journey?

6 - What will enlightenment bring to my life?

Date: ....../....../......

I am a beacon of light, illuminating my own path and that of those around me.

....

What deck called to me to be used today?

....

What is my own interpretation of each card?

....

....

....

....

....

....

....

....

....

....

....

....

....

How does this reading inspire me to take action?

....

....

Most profound message this reading?

....

Reflective thoughts & feelings	Elemental influence
....	....
....	....
....	....
....	....
....	....

Presence

This spread uses an open arm welcoming layout to symbolise the embracing nature of presence and the heartfelt openness it brings into your life. It encourages an acceptance of clarity and peace as you navigate your journey with open arms.

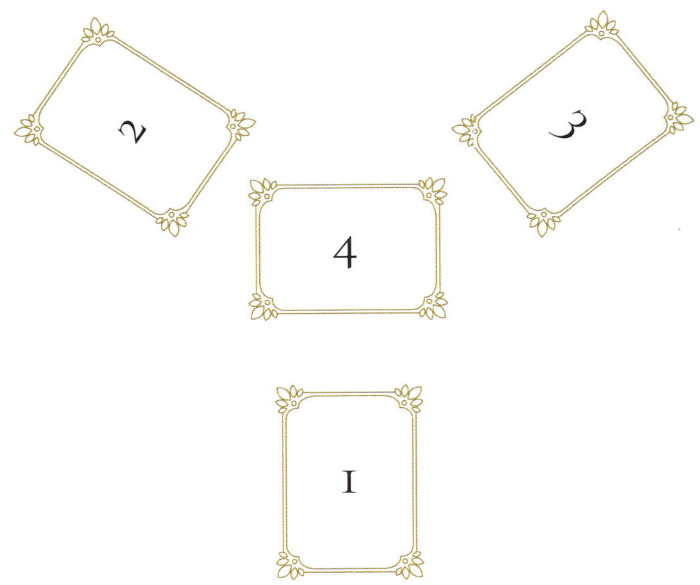

Spread questions

1 - What keeps me from being fully present?
2 - How does living in the past/future affect me?
3 - What practice can bring me into the present?
4 - How will mindfulness impact my enlightenment journey?

Date: ....../....../......

With open arms, I welcome the clarity that presence bestows upon me.

....

What deck called to me to be used today?

....

What is my own interpretation of each card?

....

....

....

....

....

....

....

....

....

....

....

....

....

How does this reading inspire me to take action?

....

....

Most profound message this reading?

....

Reflective thoughts & feelings

....
....
....
....
....

Elemental influence

....
....
....
....
....

Bright Awakening

This spread illuminates the unwavering support we offer ourselves and others, reflecting the welcoming nature of open arms. Arranged in a symphonic circle, it symbolises unity and the nurturing process of embracing each moment with compassion.

Spread questions

1 - What is currently awakening within me?

2 - How can I support my awakening process?

3 - What internal changes should I focus on?

4 - How will this awakening benefit those closest to me?

5 - What will be the highest outcome for this awakening for myself and others?

Date: ....../....../......

I am awakened to my journey, nurturing every step with love and openness.

What deck called to me to be used today?

What is my own interpretation of each card?

How does this reading inspire me to take action?

Most profound message this reading?

Reflective thoughts & feelings

Elemental influence

Inner Voice

This spread unveils the guidance of your inner voice, directing you towards clarity and alignment. Arranged in a compass rose, it symbolises direction and the steady guidance found within, helping you navigate your path with confidence.

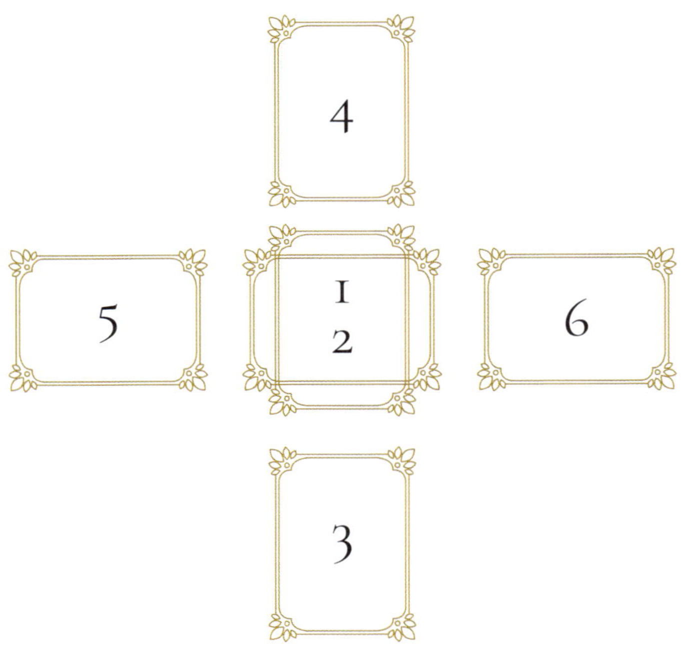

Spread questions

1 - What is my inner voice trying to tell me?

2 - What distractions are preventing me from hearing it?

3 - How can I deepen my connection to this guidance?

Extended spread

4 - What actions should I take based on this guidance?

5 - How can I begin to trust my inner guidance more?

6 - What will be the outcome of following my inner compass?

Date: ....../....../......

I trust my compass, listening to its wisdom as it leads me towards my true path.

What deck called to me to be used today?

What is my own interpretation of each card?

How does this reading inspire me to take action?

Most profound message this reading?

Reflective thoughts & feelings

Elemental influence

Universal Connection

This spread is laid in a stellar web, with each card acting as a star, revealing your potential harmonious and complex connections with the universe itself, and illuminating different facets of your universal connections.

Spread questions

1 - How can I connect more deeply with the universe?

2 - What does this look like for me?

3 - What practices can enhance my connection to the universe?

Extended spread

4 - What might be blocking this connection I desire?

5 - How does the universe communicate with me?

6 - What insights will this universal connection bring?

Date: ....../....../......

I am intricately woven into the universal tapestry, I embrace my light within it.

....

What deck called to me to be used today?

....

What is my own interpretation of each card?

....

....

....

....

....

....

....

....

....

....

....

....

....

How does this reading inspire me to take action?

....

....

Most profound message this reading?

....

Reflective thoughts & feelings

....

....

....

....

....

Elemental influence

....

....

....

....

....

Wise Unfolding

This spread helps you delve into the depths of accumulated wisdom to guide your present and future journey. Arranged in an open book layout, it symbolises the unfolding and integration of knowledge into your life's path.

Spread questions

1 - What ancient wisdom is available to me?
2 - How can I begin access and understand this wisdom?
3 - What challenges in understanding might present themselves?
4 - How can I integrate this wisdom into my daily life?
5 - What role does patience play in gaining wisdom?
6 - What transformation will occur when I embrace my wisdom?

Date: ....../....../......

With each chapter of life, I integrate wisdom's guiding light into my being.

What deck called to me to be used today?

What is my own interpretation of each card?

How does this reading inspire me to take action?

Most profound message this reading?

Reflective thoughts & feelings

Elemental influence

Divine Alignment

This spread uncovers the alignment pathways with your higher self, aiming to strengthen your connection and purpose. Arranged in an hourglass layout, it signifies the flow of time and the balance between past, present, and future alignment.

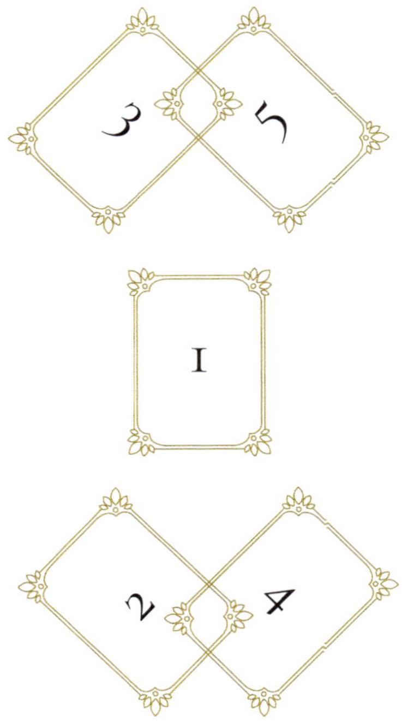

Spread questions

1 - How can I start to confidently align myself with divine will?
2 - What needs to shift within me for better alignment?
3 - What practices do I use to support my divine alignment?
4 - What signs will indicate that I am in alignment?
5 - What future blessings will divine alignment bring?

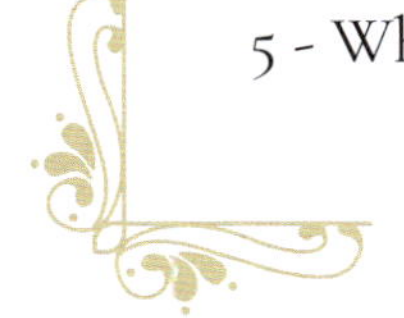

Date: ....../....../......

I align my actions with the wisdom of my soul, embracing my true path.

What deck called to me to be used today?

What is my own interpretation of each card?

How does this reading inspire me to take action?

Most profound message this reading?

Reflective thoughts & feelings

Elemental influence

This spread explores the opening of your heart and emotional growth, arranged in a half heart layout, symbolising the unfolding journey of compassion and connection.

Spread questions

1 - What is blocking my heart's awakening?

2 - How can I open my heart more fully to this awakening?

3 - What role does love play in my enlightenment journey?

4 - What will my life look like with an awakened heart?

Date: ....../....../......

I open my heart to love, allowing my emotions to flow and nurture my soul.

What deck called to me to be used today?

What is my own interpretation of each card?

How does this reading inspire me to take action?

Most profound message this reading?

Reflective thoughts & feelings

Elemental influence

Higher Connection

This spread explores the connection with your higher self, aiming to bring clarity and insight into your life's journey. Arranged in a right hand layout, it symbolises the support and guidance of your inner wisdom.

Spread questions

1 - What message does my higher self have for me?

2 - Am I connected with my higher self?

3 - How can I better connect with my higher self?

Extended spread questions

4 - What barriers must I overcome to hear my higher self?

5 - What practices or rituals will deepen this connection?

6 - What will manifest as I align with my higher self?

7 - How can my higher self guide my enlightenment journey?

Date: ....../....../......

I am connected with the highest version of myself today and at all times.

....

What deck called to me to be used today?

....

What is my own interpretation of each card?

....

....

....

....

....

....

....

....

....

....

....

....

....

How does this reading inspire me to take action?

....

....

Most profound message this reading?

....

Reflective thoughts & feelings

....

....

....

....

....

Elemental influence

....

....

....

....

....

Consciousness

This spread delves into the vast realms of your consciousness, arranged in a celestial arc layout. It symbolises the expansive nature of the mind and the journey towards greater awareness.

Spread questions

1 - What does pure consciousness mean for me?
2 - How can I achieve a state of pure consciousness?
3 - What obstacles prevent me from experiencing it?
4 - What practices can help maintain this state?
5 - How will pure consciousness transform my life?

Date: ....../....../......

I expand my consciousness embracing the limitless possibilities within me.

....

What deck called to me to be used today?

....

What is my own interpretation of each card?

....

....

....

....

....

....

....

....

....

....

....

....

....

How does this reading inspire me to take action?

....

....

Most profound message this reading?

....

Reflective thoughts & feelings	Elemental influence
....	....
....	....
....	....
....	....
....	....

Soul's Purpose

This spread assists in understanding your soul's true purpose, with intentions to illuminate the path towards fulfilling it. Arranged in a shooting star layout, it symbolises hope and direction on your journey of self-discovery and alignment.

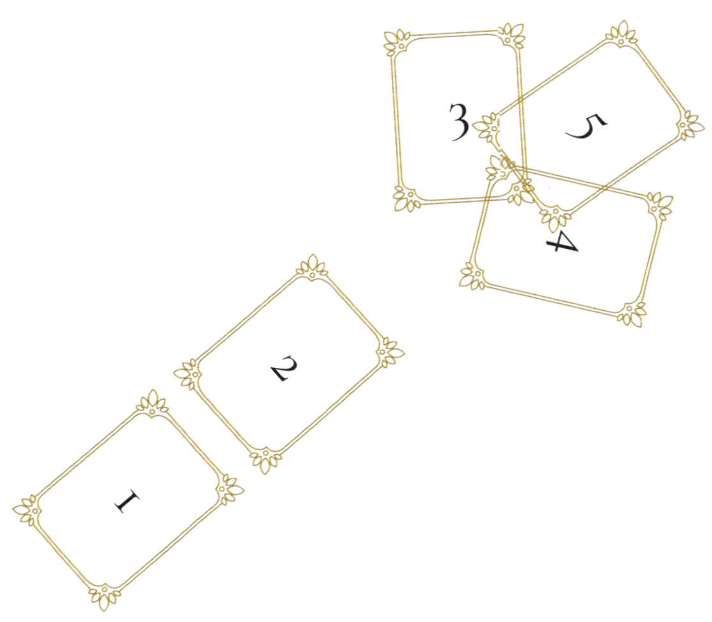

Spread questions

1 - What is my soul's true purpose?
2 - What clues in my life have guided me towards this purpose?
3 - What earthly barriers prevent me from fulfilling it?
4 - What steps can I take to align with my soul's purpose?
5 - What fulfilment will come from embracing my soul's purpose?

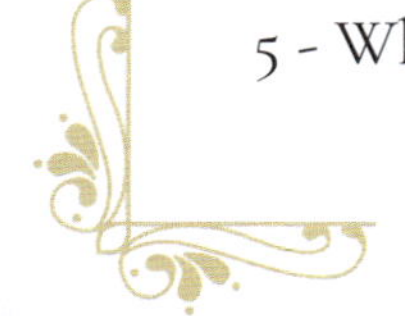

Date: ....../....../......

I am guided by the light of my soul, aligning my path with its true purpose.

....

What deck called to me to be used today?

....

What is my own interpretation of each card?

....

....

....

....

....

....

....

....

....

....

....

....

....

How does this reading inspire me to take action?

....

....

Most profound message this reading?

....

Reflective thoughts & feelings	Elemental influence
....	....
....	....
....	....
....	....
....	....

Eternal Peace

This spread encourages reflection on inner tranquility, promoting understanding and healing towards lasting peace. Arranged as zen stacking stones, symbolising the continuous journey towards serenity and balance amongst chaos.

Spread questions

1 - What is currently disrupting my inner peace?
2 - How can I restore and maintain peace within?
3 - What practices will aid me in achieving eternal peace?
4 - How will my life evolve when I reach eternal peace within?

Date: ....../....../......

I embrace tranquility within and let it guide me to eternal peace.

What deck called to me to be used today?

What is my own interpretation of each card?

How does this reading inspire me to take action?

Most profound message this reading?

Reflective thoughts & feelings

Elemental influence

Enlightenment Manifestation

This spread uncovers the facets of enlightenment you are manifesting and guides you to enhance these energies. Arranged in an Enso circle layout, it symbolises the journey of spiritual transformation, where the circle is both empty and full, reflecting the moon-mind of enlightenment and manifestation.

Spread questions

1 - What aspects of enlightenment am I already manifesting?

2 - What areas need more focus in my manifestation?

3 - How can I enhance my manifestation power?

Extended spread

4 - What beliefs must I release to manifest enlightenment?

5 - What assistance can I seek for better manifestation?

6 - What enlightenment will manifest for me as a result?

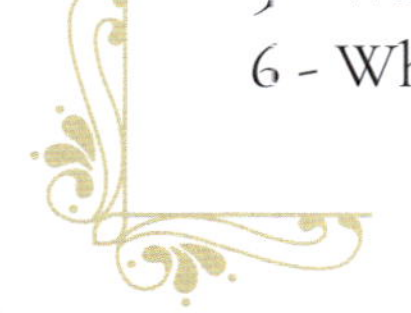

Date: ....../....../......

I embrace the infinite circle of enlightenment in every moment of my journey.

....

What deck called to me to be used today?

....

What is my own interpretation of each card?

....

....

....

....

....

....

....

....

....

....

....

....

....

How does this reading inspire me to take action?

....

....

Most profound message this reading?

....

Reflective thoughts & feelings

....

....

....

....

....

Elemental influence

....

....

....

....

....

Cosmic Awareness

This spread deepens your understanding of the universe and your place within it. Arranged in an infinity flow loop, it embodies the journey of growth and cosmic connection.

Spread questions

1 - Where am I currently in my cosmic journey?

2 - How can I elevate my cosmic awareness?

3 - What limits my current awareness?

4 - What tools can enhance my cosmic understanding?

Extended spread questions

5 - How can I apply this awareness to my everyday life?

6 - What changes will come with heightened cosmic awareness?

7 - What additional insights can aid my cosmic growth?

8 - How do I connect with the universal consciousness?

Date: ....../....../......

I expand my consciousness and the limitless potential of the cosmos within me.

....

What deck called to me to be used today?

....

What is my own interpretation of each card?

....

....

....

....

....

....

....

....

....

....

....

....

....

How does this reading inspire me to take action?

....

....

Most profound message this reading?

....

Reflective thoughts & feelings	Elemental influence
....	....
....	....
....	....
....	....
....	....

My Mirror

"My Mirror" encourages you to visualise yourself as your most enlightened self. Capturing this vivid mental image and the wisdom it embodies, imagine standing before your mirror, witnessing your powerful essence. Painting a vibrant written picture of your enlightened self, recreate this transformative personal vision in words .

Date: ....../....../......

Craft a personal affirmation inspired by your reflections on the "My Mirror" page.

....

How did visualising my whole, enlightened self feel to me today?

....

....

How do I perceive my reflection within this mirror at this moment in time?

....

....

....

....

....

In what ways has my self-perception transformed throughout this section?

....

....

....

....

....

In what ways did the recognition of my enlightened self change my expectations?

....

....

....

How does this realisation of self inspire me to take action?

....

....

Old patterns I am leaving behind	The enlightened me is...
....	....
....	....
....	....
....	....
....	....

Love Letter To My Shadow

A love letter is a beautiful way to explore self-reflection and growth. With the questions provided, use the space below to design a tarot spread representing your personal journey.

Spread questions

1 - How do I now personally define my shadow self?

2 - How well do I now recognise my inner voices and shadows?

3 - What has shaped my emotional landscape during this time?

4 - What tools has recognising my shadow given to me?

Extended spread questions

5 - How have I adapted since connecting with my shadow?

6 - What patterns have I been able to unravel and reassess?

7 - How will I be strengthened now I recognise my whole self?

8 - What was my biggest success during this period of reflection?

Date: ....../....../......

My shadow is not a part of me, it is my whole self, and I embrace all parts.

....

What deck did I wish to express gratitude to my shadow by using today?

....

What cards called to be drawn during this love letter to my shadow self?

....

....

....

....

....

....

....

....

....

What was the greatest fear I overcame when connecting with my shadows?

....

....

How am I inspired to move forward with confidence and clarity in the future?

....

....

Most profound message this reading?

....

Elements of self I had rejected	Elements of self I have discovered
....	....
....	....
....	....
....	....
....	....